Follow Me AGAIN

Recommitting to Christ's Call

Follow Me AGAIN

Recommitting to Christ's Call

SCOTT TUCKER & dARREN WALTER

n COVENANT

www.covenantpublishing.com

P U B L I S H I N G

P.O. Box 390 · Webb City, Missouri 64870
Call toll free at 877.673.1015

Library of Congress Cataloging-in-Publication Data

Tucker, Scott, 1953-
  Follow me again : recommitting to Christ's call /
Scott Tucker & Darren Walter.
     p. cm.
  ISBN 1-892435-15-2 (pbk.)
  1. Christian life—Biblical teaching. 2. Bible. N.T.
John—Criticism,
interpretation, etc. I. Walter, Darren, 1972- II.
Title.
  BS2545.C48 T83 2002
  226.5'06—dc21

                              2002005993

Acknowledgments

Scott Thanks:

There are so many people who have provided support to me as these chapters were written, and each one contributes a piece of themselves to this work. My gratitude and appreciation go to: my wife Cathy, who listened patiently to these words, offered gentle criticism and believed that God would use this project even when I forgot that He could, through your life I have learned what Godliness means, thanks for your love and support—I love you; To Darren, a gifted speaker and writer who loves God with all that is in Him and through whom God expresses His majestic truths in elegant ways—you are an enduring friend, endearing brother and excellent writing partner; To my Mom, Dad and brother Casey—Your love has made me much of who I am and your constant shoulder and unrelenting encouragement are always treasured, even when I don't stop to say thanks; to Kirk & Catrina and Anna and Dale—what a priceless gift of God your friendship is and has been, I appreciate all the times you let me share the details of this book and the details of my life with you; To the wonderful family in Christ at Myers Christian Church, who showed us what faithfulness is all about in how you live your lives—who ministered to me while God let me minister to you; and to the smiling faces and open arms that belong to my family in the Lord at Brookville Church of Christ, (especially Ed and Ruthanne Campbell, Cleamont and Gayle Moore, and Bruce and Karen Armstrong) I am looking forward to the adventure of serving God with all of you.

Darren Thanks:

I wish to thank my wife Amanda, the woman who proves to me every day that marriage is extremely under-rated. Thank you sweetheart for your constant love, support and encouragement. Whatever God does in my life Amanda, you've been His agent of encouragement, challenge and building up. Thank you, I love you. (Dance) To my dad Garry, thank you for your example of generosity and for planting the seeds of "Give it a try!" early in my growing up years. To my mom Diane, thank you for your love and way of caring. You've always made home a special place. To my sister Kara, thank you for putting up with me and for being a great friend and encourager. And to my Grandparents, Leo & Zelma, thank you for your lives of faith and trust in God's Word. Your example challenges me to be more like Christ each day. To my great family, I love you. Thank you! Special thanks also goes to Debbie Carper for her help and encouragement. Last but not least, I wish to thank Scott Tucker. You have been a friend and brother in Christ far beyond what I deserve to have. Thank you for speaking my language! Thank you for being an awesome writer and writing partner. Thank you for memories that will keep me laughing for the rest of my life. Here's to you brother, and here's to a dream come true!

Together We Thank:

The family that we were given through our time at KCC, who supported this work in its infancy—Warmest thanks to Jason and Carrie Garris, Steve Clark, Doug Hathaway, Rob and Lara Harris, Benic Hampton (in whose preaching class this

Acknowledgments

work was born), Tom Lawson, Pete Verkruyse, Charles Gresham and so many others who forever hold a place in our hearts; To Fritz Kaufman, a brother through thick and thin, but mostly thick—Thank you for your humor, warmth and love. To the brothers and sisters in Christ at Russell Springs Christian Church who helped us grow up in the Lord and whose prayers I know still flow for me and ours for you; and finally to the Lord Jesus Christ in whom we find the strength to take each new breath and the light to take each next step—We praise you that you love us so deeply, in way that we will never be able to repay—We thank you for being the Word that tells a story so compelling that it captures our hearts and captivates our imaginations, and for the guidance you provided as these words were written. We pray that you will take this offering and bless it with your Spirit so that it might change lives and win hearts to you. May all the glory flow to your throne!

Table of Contents

Preface

Many books retell the life of Christ. Why are we adding another one to the pile? Because most of us require reminders of who Jesus is and why we follow Him. We need reassurance like John the Baptist that we have picked the right Master. We forget important truths between sleeping and waking. This contemporary study of John's Gospel presents Jesus' story in ways you may never have conceived. Just maybe the way we retell Christ's story is exactly what you need to examine where you are in life's journey. Our Christian life is as fluid as a living language and we need continual reassessment of our relationship with Jesus. Have you forgotten what it was like to answer Jesus' call the first time? If He were to ask you today "Will you follow Me?" would you follow Him again?

This book is about tilting your head and causing you to rethink your commitment to Christ. Is the cost of discipleship worth it to you? Do you need to do anything differently? Do you need to repent? to retrace your steps? to get back on the right path? You are the only one who can voice your needs to your Savior. He is the only one who can judge you, or correct you, or give you hope. Our aim is to challenge you to a personal, spiritual restoration. We want you to renew your faith in the one who first touched man in the Garden of Eden.

Although we have based our stories on the *New International Version*, we have paraphrased much of the text for dramatic impact. We want you to re-see the Creator who became like us in order to show us the path back to the Father's home.

He's asking every day. Our prayer is that you choose to answer "Yes!" It's up to you to answer Christ's call . . . would you? can you? will you follow Him again?

Following the Right Voice

"For as the Father has life in himself, so he has granted the Son to have life in himself. And he has given him authority to judge because he is the Son of Man. Do not be amazed at this, for a time is coming when *all who are in their graves will hear his voice and come out*—those who have done good will rise to live, and those who have done evil will rise to be condemned. By myself I can do nothing; I judge only as I hear, and my judgment is just, for I seek not to please myself but him who sent me. If I testify about myself, my testimony is not valid. There is another who testifies in my favor, and I know that his testimony about me is valid. You have sent to John and he has testified to the truth. Not that I accept human testimony; but I mention it that you may be saved. John was a lamp that burned and gave light, and you chose for a time to enjoy his light. I have testimony weightier than that of John. *For the very work that the Father has given me to finish, and which I am doing, testifies that the Father has sent me*" (John 5:26-36, emphasis added).

Chapter One

The First Word

John 1:1-18

FOG CANDLELIGHT LOVE LETTER WISDOM MURDER COFFIN COTTON CANDY COFFEE CUP CHAMPAGNE WAR PORCH SWING THANK-YOU CHRISTMAS SONG REUNION PACING WINDOW OCEAN SUNSET KISS DINNER PARTY FIREPLACE TIME DEEP SLEEP PICNIC . . .

Words are powerful. Words have the power to change a face. They can cause a raised eyebrow, a dropped jaw, a snubbed nose. They can bring a blush, a smile, a tear.

Words are powerful. Words have the power to alter circumstances. They can keep a nation out of war, a litigant from unjustly going to jail, a child from an accident. They can produce a reformation, a willingness to give, a desire to love.

Words are powerful. Words have the power to initiate. They can start a fight, a declaration of independence, a marriage proposal. They can begin a graduation ceremony or a death sentence.

Words are powerful. Words have the power to fulfill a wish. They can mean a package has arrived, a woman has fallen in love, a mercy has been granted. They can tell of a healthy newborn, a "thank-you" deserved, a question answered.

Words are powerful. Some words have more impact and power than others do. Sometimes a word's power is found in how it's spoken. The slightest inflection or emphasis can mean the world. A letter to a lover may be completely misunderstood because the person who has written those words isn't there to say them exactly as they were intended.

A word's impact can depend on when it's spoken. There is almost nothing as useless as a word spoken too late, and nothing as priceless as a word spoken just at the right time. When a man says, "I love you" to his wife when she feels lost, it can mean everything. When he says, "I love you" in tears, with his body clinging to her cold casket, the words seem to ricochet around the empty room and echo back . . . *"too late."*

A word's power can depend on to whom the word is spoken. If the phrase, "you are free" is said to a man who is already free, it makes no difference. If it is said to a man who is on death row, it seems to get a more dramatic reaction.

A word's power can depend on who is speaking the word. If a fool says ,"follow me," you probably wouldn't. If the man with the map says, "follow me," you certainly would. If a person says, *"Let there be light,"* you probably wouldn't blink. If the God of the universe says, "Let there be light," prepare to see the darkness disappear.

Is there anything with as much impact as a word? Is there anything with as much power as a word? How long has a word been around? Long before the wordcrafters have been around. Long before Shakespeare, long before Poe, long before Hemingway, long before language, there existed a personage so indescribable, so amazing, so powerful and impacting He could only be described as *THE WORD.*

In the beginning was the Word, and the Word was with God, and the Word was God. He was with God in the beginning. Through him all things were made and without him nothing was made that has been made. in him was life and that life was the light of men. The light shines in the darkness, but the darkness has not understood it. He was in the world, and though the world was made through him, the world did not recognize him. He came to that which was his own, but his own did not receive him. Yet to all who received him, to those who believed in his name, he gave the right to become children of God . . . children born not of natural descent, nor of human decision or a husband's will, but born of God. THE WORD BECAME FLESH AND MADE HIS DWELLING AMONG US (John 1:1-14a, emphasis added).

In the beginning was THE WORD. In the beginning was the single most solitary and complete source of power and authority. As a single word can flood the mind with emotions, moods, pictures, and memories so the singleness and totality of THE WORD, floods all existence and all time with His power and impact. He has been around from the absolute beginning.

THE WORD was not only with God, He was God. He was not only on level ground with God, He was the fullness of God. Through THE WORD everything was created and crafted. THE WORD made everything that was made, probably by just speaking . . . a word.

In THE WORD is the source of life. The life of who He is has become the light of who we are. A single word spoken in a quiet room can be just as beneficial as a single candle in a dark one. And that's what happened. Like a word spoken, cutting through the silence, the light of men, THE WORD entered our dark world and shattered the night.

THE WORD, the one that was with God and was God . . . the one who has been around since the beginning . . . the one who created matter and molecules and mist and memory and mud . . . and man, THAT WORD, THE WORD, BECAME PART OF OUR WORLD AND CAME TO LIVE WITH US.

THE WORD became flesh and made His dwelling among us. Have you ever considered how bizarre that is? It's the Creator becoming the created. It's the Painter becoming the canvas. It's the Baker becoming the bread.

How do you put God in a body? How do you gel the infinite and the finite? How do you place the mind of God in a human brain? How do you fit the Spirit of God in a man's framework? It's like squeezing an elephant into a ring box. It's like getting oil and water to mix and stay mixed. Out of all impossibilities, this would seem to be most impossible. You think that's impossible? Hold on, it gets better. How do you put God in the body of an infant? You would think that if something so strange would dare happen that we would at least expect a "SUPER MAN," "A GIANT," "A HUMAN SO VASTLY DIFFERENT THAT HE WOULD BE INHUMAN," but that's not the way it happened. THE WORD came into our world as an infant . . . a helpless, defenseless infant. How do you put God in a body?

The impossible was made possible when in the courts of Heaven, the perfect WORD put on an imperfect body. The infinite and the finite were merged when the stars made a staircase that descended to a waiting world.

The God of the universe did what couldn't be done when THE WORD stepped off the throne and entered the world that He had created and held in His hand like a marble.

THE WORD BECAME FLESH AND MADE HIS DWELLING AMONG US.

It happened at conception by the Holy Spirit some months before. Now THE WORD is taking the name of Jesus on a starry night, in a town on planet earth, called Bethlehem. THE WORD came to a man and his wife, who surely were a little nervous. They weren't use to being the parents of the God of the universe. And even though they were stunned with the wonder of God, they had no idea of the impossibility that lay before them in a pile of coarse hay. They had no idea that the newborn baby that slept had been around since before time began, and had never closed His eyes, not even once, not even for a nap. As they watched the infant discover His tiny hands, they had no idea that those hands had hung the stars in the sky above them.

The First Word

A million angels singing THE WORD'S birth announcement to shepherds and a signaling star were the extent of Heaven's pageantry that night. You would think that an event like this would call for God to roll back the sky and personally tell every living soul what was about to take place, but He didn't. It was almost as if THE WORD snuck into our world like a perfect word whispers itself into a line on a page. You've been affected by it, you just don't yet realize to what extent. It crafts the direction of the story but you don't realize how until you've finished the novel.

THE WORD whispered into our world, but He shouted of the power of God.

The Word was spoken by angels in dreams, by parents in wonder, by angelic hosts in proclaiming. The Word was JESUS.

Jesus Christ, THE WORD who became flesh and made His dwelling among us. The God who became man. The Creator who became the created. The Baker that became the bread. The Savior that became the Sacrifice.

Since the first man took his first breath from the breath of God, since the first heart sounded it's first beat, since the first drop of blood coursed through an empty vein, since the first eye opened for the first time . . . all creation has waited to hear THE WORD . . . JESUS!

It must have been strange for Jesus to walk the streets of town. No one recognized Him, but He recognized everyone. Every face He encountered jogged the memory of when He fashioned that face out of nothing. Every person He passed, He remembered and knew his or her heart and mind and thoughts and motives and feelings and desires. For every person He saw, He saw the image of the Father, and the distortion of sin. Then He would remember the reason He came.

When He looked at the sea, did He remember making its

depths by pressing His fingerprint in the earth? When He walked the rocky hills, did He remember fitting the earth in His hand? When He looked at the grass and flowers and sky, did He remember coloring them with a thought? When He looked at the trees, did He remember dreaming up their existence? When He looked at the tree of the cross, did He remember the Father saying *"Son, I have something to ask of you."*

Every time we try to use our frail, crippled words to describe the things of God, we find our words lacking. For even our vast language has its limits. So how do we describe THE WORD becoming flesh? What word of ours could possibly capture the event? What collection of letters could begin to explain what God has done? Christmas?

No, that's not good enough! We need a new word don't we? I'm afraid to even begin to try to talk of what happened when THE WORD became flesh, We can't describe this with just any word. We'll have to search the vocabulary of the heart, and speak the words that only souls can utter and only a God like ours can understand.

Chapter Two

Blazing the Trail
John 1:19-34

A gentle river flowed in an out-of-place oasis that ripped through the heart of a desert wasteland, about 25 miles out of town. The voice of a man could be heard through the quick breeze that swept across the landscape. Some said the voice sounded like thunder. Some said it sounded like the echoing fire of a six-shooter, and demanded as much attention. The words he spoke bulleted through a dusty wasteland and up through the hill country.

This mysterious gunslinger had a quick eye and an even quicker finger. He took aim with his words, and never missed his target. He always aimed straight for the heart. His message was as true and clear as the river he had grown so fond of.

There were many showdowns. A high noon never went past when guns weren't loaded and words weren't fired. A thin-shelled exterior didn't stand a chance. In a matter of seconds muscles locked, holsters emptied and a barrage of bullets ricocheted through the crowd. When the deafening chaos of the bullets quieted and the dust settled, he would be the only one left standing. The only sound that could be heard were the distant echoes of the voice that thundered. Nothing moved but the stream of smoke slowly dancing from the barrel of his gun . . . today would be no different.

Follow Me Again

Out of the corner of his eye the gunslinger caught the tiny silhouette of wide-brimmed hats and wild-eyed horses perched on a hilltop two valleys away. With a signaling shot to the sky, they raced down the hillside with an avalanche of dust a length behind.

The gunslinger took his handkerchief and slowly wiped a drop of sweat from his tanned brow. His eye was fixed on the horizon. He knew what was about to happen.

The increasing rumble of the horses' hooves grew deafening as the band of horsemen barreled along the river's edge. The command of the reigns brought the determined stallions to a halt inches away from the gunslinger who stood as still as a statue.

He knew this brood of roughriders well. They had quite a reputation in these parts. This pretentious posse had become known as the "Viper Gang." They were the ones who wore the white hats, or were they whitewashed? Their intentions were as cloudy as the trail of dust they had just left behind. The gunslinger adjusted the brim of his hat to shade his eyes from the mid-day sun that hid the faces of his untimely visitors. Or perhaps their timing was just perfect.

Today, the Viper Gang was on a hunt, a hunt for answers and a hunt for identities. They had been sent by the Marshal from town back in the hill country, and they weren't returning empty-handed. These boys had tangled with the best of them, in fact they considered themselves children of the great gunslingers of old. They came from a long line of lawmen that earned the respect of their people. But now this bunch of bandits rode on the reputation of their fathers as they rode their horses.

They used the law like a lasso tying the people up in tradition. They branded the people with their mark like cattle, and some of their cattle had strayed from the herd. Their trail led straight to the gunslinger.

Blazing the Trail

The lead gunman got off his horse and moseyed over to the gunslinger and smiled a friendly smile. But the gunslinger could see the venom that dripped from his teeth. The leader of the posse asked with forked tongue and slurred speech, "Who are you, boy? What's your name? Are you the Master Gunslinger?"

He asked not only because he had been told to, but also because he wanted to know. From the time he was a boy, he had heard the stories of a gunslinger who never missed his target. As long as he could remember, the Master Gunslinger had been the talk of the town, the hearsay at every hitchin' post, and the story at every saloon.

"Are you the one? Are you the 'Master Gunslinger'?" He demanded an answer. It looked as if the gunslinger hadn't heard a word he said.

The gunslinger moved his stare from the ground to the eyes of his confused questioner. "I'm afraid you're sorely mistaken mister. I'm nothing like the Master Gunslinger. When it comes to gunslinging, I've only cleared a dusty path, but He will blaze a trail. Why, I'm not even fit to shine up His boots."

"Who are you then?" they asked again. "Give us an answer to take back to those who sent us. Are you one of the great gunslingers our Fathers spoke of?"

"Wrong again partner," the gunslinger replied, "I am the one here to stir up a little thunder. The way I see it, folks got to be ready when the Master Gunslinger rides into town. He's the one I'm waiting for too. If you've come here looking for Him, you've got the wrong man. If you think I'm a sharpshooter, then you ain't seen nothin' yet."

With that, the gunslinger blew the smoke from the barrel of his gun. He spun the six shooter around and with a flash of quick silver, it was back in his holster. The gunslinger tipped his hat, turned his back to the Viper Gang, and disappeared into the setting sun.

Follow Me Again

The next morning, the gunslinger began his day like so many before, back at the river. The gunslinger never had to beg for a crowd, but after yesterday's showdown with the Viper Gang, the crowds began to arrive even earlier than usual. No one in town knew what was going to happen, but they had come to learn that trouble followed the gunslinger like a sore back followed a barn raisin'.

Every shop in town had closed early this morning. The people expected a confrontation. What they were about to see was a legend come to life. Every eye was fixed on the trigger finger of the gunslinger as he pointed the six shooter in the air and fired a single shot. He was just about to speak, when a man slowly made His way through the crowd.

The gunslinger's look shot through the stale air and landed on this stranger who stood at the river's edge. The gunslinger didn't say a word. The silence was chilling, even in the noon-day sun. The look on the gunslinger's face could mean only one thing. The Master gunslinger had finally ridden into town. The gunslinger dropped his six shooter to the ground, partly out of amazement and partly out of surrender.

The voice that had thundered was now still and calm. The gunslinger swallowed hard and choked out a word, "This . . ." he said, pointing to the stranger, "this is the one you've been looking for, the one you've been waiting for. This is the Master gunslinger who has fought the showdown between you and sin, and He's the only one left standing."

Although the gunslinger's troubles with the Viper Gang weren't over, he would continue to point the way to the one who targets the soul and brands the heart. The crowds grew thin around the river. They had gone to follow the Master gunslinger. After that, the one who prepared the way just disappeared into the shadows, which was OK with him. He had been content to live in the shadow of a legend all along.

Blazing the Trail

The gunslinger, who some called John, had many showdowns after that. The last one, he never walked away from. Some thought the same had happened to the Master Gunslinger, who some called Jesus. But three days later He came riding back into town. The final showdown was won. And with that the Master Gunslinger rode off into the sunset.

Have you felt like a target lately? Have the bullets of temptation been flying so fast around you, you don't have time to reload. Has the deafening sound of guilt, a ricochet from the past, stopped you dead in your tracks. If so, put down your gun, you can't do it alone. You don't have to do it alone. The Master Gunslinger is the Lamb of God who takes away the sins of the world. And remember, He's coming back. Some day soon, the lamb will ride back into town on His horse for a final roundup of all that are His own.

Chapter Three

It's All in Who You Know
John 1:43-50

*H*ow many people do you know? Before you start counting, let me clarify a bit. How many people do you really know. I'm not talking about those you would recognize on the street, or that you know from work, or relatives you only see at Christmas and family reunions. I'm asking how many people you really know in a deep and meaningful way. I'm guessing the number is pretty small.

Take a moment to let that soak in. Think of all the people to whom you'll say "Hi" or "How are you?" through the course of a day. Think also of how little you truly know about them. Right now on planet Earth, there are about six billion people. Chances are that, in the course of your day, you've run into more than one of them. We have a great deal of contact with other people, but we rarely involve ourselves in each other's lives.

Think about all the faces that you see each day. Behind every one of those faces is a story. Some are exciting, some amazing and others tragic. Mostly, those hidden stories will remain that way, hidden and untold. Why? Because we invest so little of our time into knowing others, I mean really getting to know them.

What about this question? How many people really know

you? This question may be even more difficult to answer than the first. Is there actually anyone who truly knows you?

If there are those who really know us, its because they have seen us in our worst and best moments. These people we gladly call our friends; and a true one is most definitely hard to come by. The people whom we love the most and know the best and who love and know us in return are those who have been genuinely interested in us and have spent a lot of time learning and understanding who we are.

Think of your best moments. In your mind look around the scene at the people who are there. Probably there are certain faces that keep popping up. These certain people are always there patting backs, shaking hands, sharing laughs, and giving smiles.

What about when life was at its worst? Perhaps those same people are there. In almost every memory, they are still there giving hugs, drying tears, holding hands, and saying prayers. In our best and worst moments and all the days in between, those we can count on mean the most to us. Where would we be without our friends? Isn't it wonderful that there are people we know in this life who want to know us.

It was a friend who first told Nathanael about a man who would forever change his life. Three days after Jesus had been baptized in the Jordan River, He decided to leave for Galilee with His two new followers, Andrew and Simon Peter. Along His way there, He ran into a man named Philip, who like Peter and Andrew was from Bethsaida. Jesus' words to him were simple and direct, "Follow me." Apparently Philip's response was equally as direct.

The very next thing that the Scripture portrays Philip doing after deciding to follow Jesus, is to go and find his friend,

Nathanael, so he can share the great news with him. Philip came to him and said, "We have found the one Moses wrote about in the Law, and about whom the prophets also wrote — Jesus of Nazareth, the son of Joseph."

What a great friend. When I hear good news, the first thing I do is tell my closest friends. It doesn't seem that good things really happen unless they know about them. This was the case between Philip and Nathanael. Even when Nathanael protested in wonder about what good thing could come from Nazareth, Philip just told him to come and take a look for himself.

As the pair approached this stranger, He began to speak. He turned and looked Nathanael straight in the eyes and said, "Here is a true Israelite, in whom there is nothing false."

Nathanael must have been flattered by these very kind words, but he was also puzzled. These two had never met before. "How do you know me?" Nathanael asked.

Jesus' response was nothing short of amazing. "I saw you while you were still under the fig tree before Philip called you." Now keep in mind that the first time the name "Jesus of Nazareth" had entered Nathanael's ears was when Philip sought him out. Even before Nathanael knew about Jesus at all, Jesus knew everything about him.

If you had asked Nathanael how many people really knew him that day, he would have definitely said at least one. One man knew him better than anyone else, even his best friend Philip. One man knew him intimately before Nathanael ever heard His name. One man was able to look past his exterior and read the story of his heart.

Nathanael's response was one of wonder and of immediate faith. Then Nathanael declared, "Rabbi, you are the Son of God; you are the King of Israel." It's not every day that you meet a total stranger who knows you better than you know yourself. Only one powerful encounter like this is needed to realize that if Jesus goes to the trouble of knowing us so deeply, then we owe it to Him to return the favor.

If you answered the question earlier that there were few people who really knew you, why do you think that is? Part of the answer may lie in the fact that we are afraid to let people read our hearts like an open book. There are too many hidden things, too much we are uncomfortable with to truly open up with others.

So instead, we hide behind masks that look like us but show nothing of who we really are. We long to be known, but are convinced that the truth about us would drive everyone away.

It's often true that in relationships with others, how much we know each other depends on how much we allow ourselves to be known. But what about with Jesus? Before He and Nathanael ever met, Jesus knew his heart because he had been able to see deeply into it. Of Nathanael, Jesus said that there was nothing false in him. How true is that for each of us?

If you are like me, there are far too many skeletons in your spiritual closet. So we tuck them further away hoping that no one will ever find out, that no one will ever know us so completely as to uncover them. But when it comes to our relationship with Jesus, all of those things are laid out in the open, in plain view right from the start.

Sure He saw purity when He looked into Nathanael's heart, but He saw the deceit in Judas, He saw the betrayal in Peter, He saw the doubt in Thomas and He also saw the potential for the kingdom in each one.

Maybe we are afraid to get to know Jesus because there are too many dark places inside of us that we don't want to be revealed. What we forget is that Jesus already knows us better than any other, we just have to respond in faith and obedience like Nathanael.

When you get to know more about Jesus, I think you'll find that your earthly friendships will grow in intimacy also. In fact, in Heaven when sin no longer holds us back we shall know fully, even as we are fully known (1 Corinthians 13:12). But for now, don't be afraid to trust in the one who knew your good and your bad but died for you anyway. And if you think that being really known by someone is great, then hold on . . . Jesus says, "You shall see greater things than that."

Chapter Four

Details, Details
John 2:1-11

*L*ittle things mean a lot. Life isn't made up of one big event after another, but rather small details, most of which you will never remember. Sometimes it's those "little things" that stand out the most . . . a smile from a stranger, a note of encouragement, an expression of thanks, the smell of Thanksgiving dinner filling the house, a warm day, your favorite song on the radio, a call just to say "hi," a hug from your kids, being with good friends.

The big event of life is most clearly a success when each detail works together. A wedding is the perfect example. It's a big event held together by a string of details. The bride debates for hours, rummaging through a blizzard of white wedding gowns. You can tour a countryside of flowers trying to assemble just the right bouquet. How many layers on the cake? When will the pictures be taken? What should be served at the reception?

The ceremony must be perfect. The right words at the proper time. Every "t" crossed, every "i" dotted, every candle lit. All the pressure of planning so many details can push you right over the threshold! You are bound to lose your cool. You are encouraged to lose a few tears. But whatever you do, don't lose the wedding rings!

When everything does fall into place . . . when all the

details fit together . . . when the ceremony is complete . . . and the music and laughter start . . . then a calm contentment settles around you and you are reminded how thankful you are for the little things in life.

"Wasn't that ceremony just lovely?" "They make such a great couple."

Every detail is discussed over cake. . .

"Isn't this food delicious." "Is there any more wine?"

Uh oh. The one detail that slipped through the cracks, not enough wine. Mary gets up from the table, empty glass in hand, to see for herself. She looks in every jar. The embarrassing rumor is true, not a drop left.

Weddings like the one in Cana of Galilee could last for a week or more. Today, bringing the details of a few hours together is stressful enough. Imagine a week-long wedding. Imagine the mountain of details, and wine was certainly an essential detail.

Friends and relatives would travel for days to share in the celebration. After miles in the dust and heat, they would be thirsty for some good wine and some good conversation. Besides, there were more toasts to be made, more glasses to be raised, more celebrating to be done.

This detail needed to be fixed and fast, but there was no corner store handy, no winepress nearby. Mary didn't want the host or the happy couple to be embarrassed, or to bother them with the problem. Today was too important. She decided to share the problem with the one person in the room who would know what to do.

Jesus saw her making her way through the crowd. Mary normally would have stopped to talk a dozen times along the way. But the further she waded through the gathering of guests, the more empty glasses she saw, and the more deter-mined she became.

Jesus could see there was a problem and Mary needed a solution. "They have run out of wine," she whispered under her breath.

Even though Mary knew that if anybody could fix it Jesus could, he really hadn't intended to perform any miracles or fix any disasters that day. "Dear woman, why are you involving me? My time hasn't come," as if to say "I will serve no wine before My time."

Mothers have a way of getting their way, especially when it comes to their children. He could have said no, but then again how could He? This was His mother. These were His friends. This was a big event and an important detail. "Do whatever He says," Mary told the servants.

Jesus pointed to six large water jars and asked that they be filled with water. They filled them to the brim. "Now draw some out," He said, "and take it to the master of the banquet." The servant came to the head table and left almost unnoticed. But this newly transformed wine did not go unnoticed, it was the best he had ever tasted.

Who knows at what point the water in the glass ceased to be water and miraculously became wine. That's a minor detail. The real significance was Jesus' concern for His friends. He knew that this little thing would make a big difference to them. Jesus knows the little things are important to you, too.

Sometimes we only bring before God the major events in life. Hospital waiting rooms are full of people who only talk to God about big things. It's not uncommon for people to seek God when they are certain their resources are exhausted, when the circumstance is too big for them to manage, too big for them to control.

When creditors come knocking but the opportunities don't . . . when your spouse becomes a stranger and one of you packs your bags . . . when a memory is all that's left of a life that has come and gone . . . certainly God is there for us in those times. However, He is also there waiting to help us with the smallest of concerns.

Don't believe God is interested in small details? Take a walk outside. Look at the veins in a leaf. Listen to the songs of birds and crickets. Examine your fingerprints. Run your fingers through your hair, God has numbered every strand. Don't tell me God's not interested in detail. He is the God of details. He is interested in how your day went. He cares about your feelings. He wants to hear what's on your mind.

Isn't it nice to know that Jesus is concerned with even the small details of our lives? The wedding party was small in comparison to the crowds that would later follow. Soon He would feed thousands. He would heal the sick and raise the dead before massive audiences, but it was here that His glory was first revealed and the disciples put their faith in Him. Could it be that Jesus was hesitant to perform this first miracle because He knew it was the first link in a chain of events that would lead to the cross?

Jesus' love and concern for the small details of life flowed as freely as the wine He made at the wedding that day. Jesus' love and concern for your greatest need, a Savior, flowed as freely as the blood shed on the cross. The motivations were the same, the deepest concern for our every need.

Jesus, who suffered great humiliation, cared about a bride and groom's potential embarrassment. The one who holds our eternity in His hands also wants to hold our hand.

The Savior who moved Heaven and earth for you also loves

Details, Details

you enough to be moved by your slightest tear. God is in the details.

The big picture of life is made up of a million tiny brush strokes: small details that by themselves seem insignificant. But in the hands of the artist, all the details come together, the picture is complete.

Chapter Five

Two Birthdays
John 3:1-21

*T*he streets were dark. A single light up ahead cast dense shadows across their path as they walked. This was not the best hour for a stroll, but tonight they had little choice. To calm their fears, they buried themselves in conversation and moved at a brisk pace toward the light. The faint glow revealed the tattered houses at their side, long since condemned. A few junk cars sat abandoned on the street. Their pulses raced and their feet did the same. The sooner they were out of here, the better.

They were almost to the light and were preparing to round the corner when a loud clanging noise behind them stopped them dead in their tracks. They quickly turned around to check it out when a voice to their left growled, "Give me all your money, now!" A man masked by a hooded jacket and the shadows grabbed the woman and threw her against the car. She resisted and lunged at the attacker, knocking him slightly off balance. Suddenly, a gleam of light streaked across something in his hand. He had a gun. He was just about to take a shot at the woman when her companion jumped onto the attacker. A shot rang out down the alley. The attacker ran off into the shadows as the man's body fell limp to the ground. He had been shot in the chest.

Follow Me Again

By the time the woman was able to call for help, it was too late. The man was pronounced dead at the scene. He had taken a bullet to the heart and died almost immediately. Except for a scratch on her forehead, the woman was fine.

A few days later, a reporter from a local television station came by to talk to the woman. With an abundance of tears she retold the story of what had happened. "I can't believe it. He gave his life to save mine." She said, "I would have been the one shot by that gun if it hadn't been for him. You know my birthday isn't until May, but I can celebrate it today. You see, I've been given two birthdays. One was when my parents gave me life and the other has just passed, when he gave me life again."

That night would loom large in her memory. Every year she would indeed, in a private way, celebrate two birthdays. She gathered in May with her family and friends to eat cake and open presents. But she was given a new birthday. Her life, it seemed, started all over again that night and she would never be the same. Every year, around this time, she remembers how her life was changed forever by the selfless act of her friend.

The streets were dark. A single light up ahead cast dense shadows across the path as he walked. This was not the best hour for a stroll, but tonight he had little choice. His mind had pondered many questions over the last few months and tonight he just had to know. He was a faithful man who loved God and wanted to do what was right. For decades now, he had faithfully followed God and his religion. His dedication coupled with years of studying the Law had led him into a rather prestigious position. He was a Pharisee and a member of the ruling council of the Jews.

He took his position very seriously. Not just anyone could

achieve this high standing. He also knew being on the Sanhedrin was more than just position, it was also a responsibility. People counted on him to have answers and to know the beliefs of his people better than anyone else. At the core of those beliefs was the ever-present hope that Messiah would come. How his heart burned for Messiah. Wouldn't it be the most wonderful gift of all if the Messiah were to come during his lifetime.

Perhaps it was this burning desire to see Messiah that dragged him by his curiosity out into the Jerusalem streets in the middle of the night. He became lost in his thoughts as he walked. Could this man be the deliverer of Israel? There had certainly been a number of wondrous miracles that had happened by His hand. Could this man really be God's answer to all his years of praying? Or was he just being a foolish old man whose fancies had overtaken his common sense?

He looked ahead at the place they were to meet and saw Jesus standing there. Nicodemus was the first to speak, "Rabbi, we know that you are a teacher who has come from God. For no one could perform the miraculous signs you are doing if God were not with him."

I don't know what Nicodemus was hoping Jesus' response would be, but I would be willing to assume it was not what he heard. Jesus' words were exact and to His point. "I tell you the truth," He said, "no one can see the kingdom of God unless he is born again."

Nicodemus replied perhaps out of confusion, perhaps out of wonder, "How can a man be born when he is old? Surely he cannot enter a second time into his mother's womb to be born!"

Scripture would seem to indicate in the few instances in which Nicodemus is mentioned, that he was at least sympathetic to Christ and His ministry. Was he a follower? Tradition indicates that eventually he was, but it really is impossible to know.

One thing is for sure. If indeed he was a devout Jew devoted to God more than to his title, then he would have deeply desired to be a part of God's kingdom if the Messiah were at hand. So when Jesus' response was that a person had to be born again to see God's kingdom, Nicodemus was at a loss.

You see, Nicodemus was an old man and being born again was something of a problem for him. He certainly could not enter his mother's womb again. A new physical birth was unattainable. He most likely had become quite set in his ways. A new spiritual birth was improbable.

Perhaps you have walked a mile in Nicodemus' shoes. You are interested in who Jesus is and what He is all about. You are curious about this "teacher who has come from God." The problem is that, like Nicodemus, you have put in a lot of hours on the time clock of life and great big changes don't come very easily to you.

Oh, but wouldn't it be incredible if somehow you could get a brand new start. But it's very uncomfortable to start all over again. Just ask Nicodemus, or even his ancestor Abraham. New starts are hard to come by. The woman in the beginning story got her new start, but at a terrible price . . . the life of a friend. But, dare I say it, so do we.

It may sound cliché to us, but the truth is that Jesus gave His life voluntarily so that people like Nicodemus and you and me could have a brand new birth. Let me be clear. A new birth means a new start, a new lease on life, but it is also so much more than that. Being born again is more than just fancy religious terminology, it is an accurate and beautiful picture of what happens to people when Christ transforms their lives.

When we are born physically, we completely change our surroundings. We move from the water of the womb to the air of the hospital room. Our nourishment now comes through our mouths rather than an umbilical cord. We rely on blankets for warmth rather than the god-designed shelter of the mother. Being born, moving from the womb to the world, means that much of what is true about our lives fundamentally changes.

One thing, however, remains constant. We are born in the flesh from the flesh. Our bodies are patterned after those of our parents. There certainly may be differences, but for the most part a baby is very much like his parents. One of the most common remarks that people make to parents about a new baby is how similar the little one is to the mom or dad. "He's a doll. He has your eyes you know." "My, oh my, he has your nose and your wife's smile." "He's going to have his dad's chiseled jaw." "Oh, she's adorable. She looks just like you."

Jesus says in verse six that "Flesh gives birth to flesh, but the Spirit gives birth to spirit." Babies have no choice but to reflect their nature. They are human beings, made by two other human beings. They exhibit the physical characteristics of their parents. No one mistakes a baby for something else. Their identities are clear. They are people. They are mirrors of their makers.

However, when it comes to our spirits, we are at the beginning of the birth canal. With babies, no matter how desperately they want to leave the womb, they can't do it on our own. The process must take place. Birth cannot happen without the actions of the mother's body. Spiritually, the same is true. We are as hopeless as an old man trying to be born again. We can't do it on our own.

If we are to become spiritual beings we must be born through spiritual means. Only the Spirit gives birth to spirit.

43

The change is as drastic as moving from the womb to the world. To participate in this life, our mother had to give us birth. To participate in life eternal, we must rely on Jesus to give us a new birth.

One difference in the spiritual birth is that we have a part to play in the process. We have to believe. Belief is the act of conception in the spiritual birth. From there Jesus takes care of the rest. "For God so loved the world that he gave his one and only Son, that whoever believes in him shall not perish but have eternal life."

God gave us His Son. Jesus died so that we might have a new birth . . . a new life. When we are born physically, we reflect our nature. We live and exist in flesh. After our spiritual birth through Christ, we now have a new nature (Acts 2:38; Galatians 3:26-29). In the spiritual birth, because of Christ, we become perfected in the eyes of God. Again, we mirror our Maker.

When people look at babies, they see traces of their parents. When the world looks at a Christian, they should see traces of the Heavenly Father. In Christ, we too can celebrate two birthdays. One when we were given physical life, and another when through the selfless act of a Friend we were given life all over again.

Following the Right Teacher

Among the crowds there was widespread whispering about him. Some said, "He is a good man." Others replied, "No, he deceives the people." But no one would say anything publicly about him for fear of the Jews. Not until halfway through the Feast did Jesus go up to the temple courts and begin to teach. The Jews were amazed and asked, "How did this man get such learning without having studied?" Jesus answered, "*My teaching is not my own. It comes from him who sent me. If anyone chooses to do God's will, he will find out whether my teaching comes from God or whether I speak on my own.* He who speaks on his own does so to gain honor for himself, but he who works for the honor of the one who sent him is a man of truth; there is nothing false about him" (John 7:12-18, emphasis added).

Chapter Six

Wishing Well
John 4:1-29

Have you ever been thirsty, I mean really thirsty? It's mid July. The high today was ninety seven. On your way back home from work, where the air conditioner just wasn't working, you visualize that icy can of Coke waiting for you in your fridge. You burst into your sub zero kitchen and indulge.

Have you ever been thirsty? Maybe you've just finished a basketball game in a stuffy, sweaty gym, where the air was so thick you could cut it with something as dull as your sneakers. You plow through the place like a tank. Nothing stands between you and the water fountain. The people behind you get impatient. Although you have lost all track of time as you slurp down the cold water in gulps, the people at your back have been keeping perfect time, and they don't care to remind you that your time is up.

Have you ever been thirsty? Maybe you've just finished working in the hay field or the cattle barn all day. The day is over and you're thirsty. You're so parched that you can barely speak. You wonder if your thirst will ever be quenched. The dry dust of a hard day's work in the field covers your throat. You'd do anything to get a glass of water, wouldn't you? Even though your body hurts and you're tired, the one thing on your mind is water . . . quenching your thirst. Have you ever been thirsty, I mean really thirsty?

Every day was practically the same for her. Get up at the crack of dawn to see her "significant other" off to work, hand him his briefcase and a sack lunch, kiss him on the cheek and watch him walk out the back door. She knew he didn't really love her, not with the deep, sacrificing kind of love she wanted anyway. She also knew that one day he would leave for the office, and that he'd never come back. But for now, he was all she had.

Her life consisted of him and countless daily errands. This morning was no different from any other. She had to get to the store, make a deposit at the bank, go to the well, clean the house, and then start thinking about supper. She thought about how boring her life and routine were as she slung her purse over her arm in disgust, and followed it with two water pots, balanced on each shoulder like they were sitting on a shelf. She was a reasonably young woman, mid 30s. She was attractive, but her eyes were aged with pain, and filled with the worry of too many sleepless nights.

"I can't believe it's so hot out here already this morning!" "she said as she walked through town. She had learned to talk to herself to avoid hearing the casual whispers of the towns-people. Some looked through her like she was transparent. Some stared. Some didn't even bother to look. Her mental conversation never seemed to drown out the snide comments of the crowds. A group of women behind her added their personal commentary. "Watch your husbands ladies, there she goes." "What is this, number five or six?" "I wonder who the 'lucky' man is this month?" She just kept walking.

Trying to ignore them, she looked down at her dusty feet

moving through the 100-degree sand. She was tired, tired of the humiliating walk through town every morning. Tired of nobody caring and nobody showing any hope, or a way out. She was tired, and by the time she reached the well she was thirsty. The morning sun in Sychar can pound down hard and hot.

The sound of chattering busybodies quieted behind her and in front of her she could see the well of Jacob at a distance. Nothing about the well had changed since yesterday morning, just like nothing in her life had changed . . . not for the better at least. She sat her water pots down. She drew some water from the well, and took a drink, The water tasted good.

She positioned herself on one of the over-sized, dirty stones that cluttered the area. For a few moments she stared at the water pots. She knew they'd be empty after supper and tomorrow morning would find her back here at the well; probably tired again, probably feeling like the dirt she now played in with her sandal. And more than likely just as thirsty as she was that morning.

She took a third gulp from her small drinking jar, and looked up. She saw a stranger sitting under a tree, trying to soak in some shade. He looked like a Jew. She didn't let Him know that He had just startled her, and didn't waste any time in getting back to her work filling water pots.

"Will you give me a drink of water?" the Stranger asked. She reached down the well for the rope and bucket submerged out of sight. With her head sticking down into the opening of the well she said, "Are you as blind as you are thirsty, stranger? I'm a Samaritan, I didn't think you Jews talked to our kind."

The Stranger replied, "If you only knew about God's gift and who I am, you'd be asking me for water instead of trying to fish it out of that well. The water I could give you is living water." Almost not paying attention to Him the woman pulled up the bucket and poured some water into her drinking jar. She handed it to the stranger without looking at Him. "You're going to need something to draw with, this well isn't shallow you know. And, what do you mean living water, this well has always been full and more than adequate for what we've needed."

The man answered, "This well is a lot emptier than you think it is. Everyone who drinks this well water will be thirsty again, just like you are thirsty from your walk here every morning. But the water I give, the living water I speak of, will quench your thirst for eternity. What's more, there will be springs of life and love gushing in your soul."

With that announcement the woman perked up. "Sir, where do you find it, and could I have some of this never-ending water. I hate coming to this well every morning!"

"Certainly," He said, "Go get your husband and I'll tell you all about it." Her head dropped and she returned to her work, "I don't have a husband."

"You're right," the Man said," You've had five husbands, and the man you're living with now probably talks more with his secretary than with you." She started crying. She had been searching all her life for a satisfying relationship. It's not like she hadn't tried to make it work. Five husbands ago, she would have given anything for love, devotion, intimacy. But now five relationships later she was more empty than when she started.

Although she had someone to watch the evening news with in silence she was more alone than ever before. She felt spent and used and useless. She had looked everywhere and tried everything, but nothing worked and she was at the end of her rope. She was alone and hopeless . . . and still thirsty.

Wishing Well

Have you ever been thirsty, I mean really thirsty? Have you ever been as thirsty as the woman at the well? So thirsty that you searched everywhere for fulfillment? So thirsty that you tried everything, did everything you could, exhausted all your resources? Have you gone to Jacob's well in search of quenching, all the while not noticing the stranger under the shade tree? Did you fail to notice the God-water that was on tap? Have you ever left the spring of forgiveness, righteousness, and Godliness, only to do things your way . . . to dig your own well. The water isn't as good is it? It's not as refreshing is it? Water found with our strength, and power, never is.

Jeremiah 2:13 says, "My people have committed two sins: They have forsaken me, the spring of living water, and have dug their own cisterns, broken cisterns that cannot hold water." Have you forsaken the spring of living water? Have you dug your own cistern, your own well . . . only to find your liquid treasure leaking out all over every thing? Have you tasted the bitter water of doing things your way, in your time, following your agenda, rather than God's? Have you run from the very source of your life . . . from the spring of living water?

Have you told God with your actions that you were going to do things your way? Are you drawing water from the deadly well of apathy toward Christ and His Word? Do you find yourself at the well of physical relationships . . . digging and scraping the bottom? Are you trying to quench your thirst with trendy friends, fancy cars, a starting position on the team, all the right clothes?

Oh sure, you thought it would do the trick but you found nothing but dry ground at the bottom of your well. Your bucket has hit the bottom of life's dusty well hasn't it? Your wit, your rapport with people, your rock solid image won't hold up much longer . . . not without the endorsement of the well-keeper.

Is any of this making you thirsty? Are you thirsty for living water? Do you want real life back again? Do you want that thirst quenched with living water? If so, then the silhouetted picture of Jacob's well, a caring Man, and a crying woman beg your attention. She was thirsty too. She had done things her own way long enough, and she was parched. She didn't like the way she had done things. She tried to forget about her fruitless, drought-stricken life, but Jesus had to go and remind her of the dry, lifeless way she was just getting by. He just had to bring up the five mistakes of her past. He just had to remind her of the man who was now in some office building down-town, who was probably contemplating leaving her the next morning.

She didn't want to talk about her bleak and dusty history of doing things her way. She was so ashamed of it all. The sun illuminated the tears that streamed down her face. She looked up at the Stranger. She had never seen such compassion in a man's eyes . . . certainly in none that she had ever known.

The woman nervously dried her eyes and tried to change the subject. He obliged her for a moment. He knew she was hurting and thirsty for life. He saw through her nice outfit and made-up face into her parched and dry heart. She needed a drink . . . a drink of living water. In another attempt to avoid the subject, she stumbled upon it. "When Messiah comes, He will make everything clear to us." Jesus answered, "I am He."

They sat and talked for a while longer about life and about being thirsty. Jesus told her of the refreshing water of forgive-ness and how her past could be forgotten and forgiven. He told her about the one "relationship" that really mattered . . .

her relationship to God. Jesus had made her a new woman. Jesus had gushed life into the dry cavern of her existence. He had told her about living water . . . God's gift.

She was so excited, she left her water jars behind. She ran right back into the village and told everyone about Jesus and what He had said. She even told those old busybodies about the clean water of forgiveness and new life. She had been sipping from a half-empty cup of muddy water, but now she had found the source of crisp, clean, living water . . . and she just kept drinking.

Have you ever been thirsty . . . I mean really thirsty?

Chapter Seven

Real Soul Food
John 6:1-35

*T*here are at least two subjects that will start a conversation with most anyone. We're not talking about asking someone how they are or what they think of the weather. We are talking about subjects that will start people speeding down the conversation superhighway. The problem is these two subjects will put you on the fast lane to strong opinions and the freeway to flared tempers.

"What are they?" you ask. Well, don't take our word for it. The next time you are in a crowd of people itching for a topic, just bring up religion or politics. Almost everyone is either afraid of one or an expert on the other. Since most of what we write about is religion, we'll yield the floor to politics for a moment.

Unless you are determined to have no contact with the outside world, it's likely you'll hear something about politics on a regular basis. There appears to be no end to the constant battle between political parties, left and right, pro and con, right and wrong. In essence, politics has become a tug-of-war. Issues and images, principles and priorities, careers and constituents are thrown to the lions in the political arena every day.

In the midst of all this confusion there remains one political certainty. Candidates go to great lengths to secure our vote. It's still illegal to buy votes, but millions of dollars are spent on campaigns to let the public know what each candidate offers.

"Elect me, and I'll lower your taxes."

"Elect me, and I'll make your voice heard in government."

"Elect me, and I'll push education reforms and improvements."

"Elect me, and I'll see that your section of town gets special attention."

"Elect me, and I'll make jobs more available in your community."

"Elect me, and I'll give you this colorful button, with my name on it, to wear."

What's that in front of your face? A carrot being dangled on a string? We pledge our vote for a handful of sparkling promises. We trade in our allegiance for bobbles and trinkets.

Makes you a little upset doesn't it? It almost makes you feel victimized. But it's been happening to us since we were kids riding in the grocery cart. You begged for the cereal you hated, just to get the cheap, little toy in the bottom of the box. It's incredible to see how easily trinkets and toys can grab our attention and sway our allegiance. We pass over the important things to get to the trinket. We would rather hold a four-leaf clover for luck than make positive things happen. We give to charities to get the tax write-off. Nothing mobilizes our society like the word "free."

Free trinkets draw crowds. Everyone has their Ph.D. in bargain hunting and no price is too high when it comes to a free lunch. Anywhere you find something for nothing, you can find the crowd not too far behind.

Hot on the trail of the trinket, the crowd followed Him from what seemed to be one magic show to the next. The blind were seeing. The lame were walking. Most importantly though, the crowd was being entertained. Last week someone was raised from the dead, and you didn't even need a ticket. Who knew what would happen today? You can bet your bottom dollar that they were betting theirs on something bigger and better happening today than the day before.

The grass made great bleachers for the crowd of thousands that day. Have you ever noticed that there is a food court in every mall. That's because bargain hunting makes you hungry. They had come for a show that day, but wouldn't you know it, they had forgotten to pack their lunch. Little did they know, the lunch they were about to eat would be the show.

Have you ever asked a question for which you already knew the answer? That's what Jesus did. He turned to Philip and asked, "Where are we going to buy enough bread to feed a crowd like this?" Philip had little response after digging in his pocket and finding himself more than a few silver pieces short. Jesus already had in mind what he was going to do.

Andrew wasn't sure what difference it would make, but he spoke up anyway, "Here is a boy with five small barley loaves and two small fish, but how far will they go among so many?" Andrew knew that if anyone could take a handful and make a stomach full for all these people, it was Jesus.

Jesus told Andrew to have all the people sit down. Those hoping to be amazed and entertained took their seats for the big show. Jesus was the center of attention in this outdoor drama as He took the young boy's lunch and gave thanks. The back row of the crowd scanned the thousands in front of them and saw the front row being fed.

What was He doing? Is He honestly trying to feed this crowd with a few loaves and fish? Oh sure, the first two or three people might get a bite but what about audience member number 5,000? But as Jesus went from person to person, they kept taking food from His hands. Jesus was using strange ingredients for a meal. He was making fish and bread out of thin air.

The crowd was amazed. In no time, the miracle made its way up the hillside. Bread and fish were everywhere. People didn't know what to do but laugh. Laugh and sing and dance and eat . . . and eat . . . and eat. Talk about a free lunch. They had seen Jesus do wonderful things for some, the sick and the needy, but never before had He done so much for so many at one time. After baskets of leftovers had been collected, their stomachs were full, but they hadn't had their fill of Jesus.

Jesus was remarkable. They had never been a part of anything like this. If an opinion poll were taken that day, Jesus' popularity would have been at 100%. What if every day with Jesus was like this. No more beggars on the street. Devotion to God would be so much easier. A chicken in every pot. A man like that ought to be king. Nothing stirs up a crowd like religion and politics. Put them both together and you get a winning combination . . . like fish and bread.

The crowd held a spontaneous election. The vote was unanimous. They decided to volunteer Jesus to be their king. The Scripture says, "Jesus, knowing that they intended to come and make him king by force, withdrew again to a mountain by himself." It's no wonder Jesus left the crowd. His kingship wasn't up for a vote.

Around nightfall, the disciples set sail for Capernaum across the lake. No doubt they were flabbergasted with what Jesus had done that day. Their stomachs, still full, reminded them that Jesus had mastered the impossible. It wasn't long until He reminded them of that again when, three miles away from shore, Jesus walked up beside the boat and got in. Immediately the boat reached Capernaum's shore. As Jesus and the disciples were stepping out of the boats, the crowd was stepping into boats on the other side of the lake. Jesus had gotten away from them once, but they were determined it wouldn't happen again. They wanted their king, plus it was about time for breakfast.

When they finally found their good luck charm, He was on the other side of the lake with the disciples. Half frustrated and half amazed, they asked, "Teacher, when did you get here?"

Jesus did not tell them how He got there but instead, why they came. "You're chasing after Me, not because you are hungry for God but because you are hungry for the free food that I give you. Why are you making all this effort for food that will spoil? Instead, work for food that feeds your soul and nourishes your spirit forever. The Son of Man will give you this. He is God's certified chef."

"What do we have to do to get this food?" They asked.

Jesus explained, "Your part is simple, just believe in the one God has sent."

"Your part is simple too," they said. "Just give us a sign and we'll believe. What will you do? God provided bread from heaven for our forefathers when he sent them manna. Now that's a sign!" The crowd asked Jesus for the sign that He had already given them. They had apparently forgotten how they had gorged themselves on five loaves and two fish just across the lake.

Jesus reminded them, "It wasn't Moses who gave them bread from heaven, it was my Father. He gives you the true bread from heaven. This true bread from God isn't manna, it is he who comes down from heaven who gives life to the world."

"Sir," they insisted, "from this point on, we want you to give us this bread."

"You're missing the point," Jesus clarified, "I am the bread of life. He who comes to me will never go hungry, and he who believes in me will never be thirsty. But as I told you, you have seen me and still you do not believe. All that the Father gives me will come to me, and whoever comes to me I will never drive away. For I have come down from heaven not to do my will but to do the will of him who sent me. And this is the will of him who sent me, that I shall lose none of all that he has given me, but raise them up at the last day. For my Father's will is that everyone who looks to the Son and believes in him shall have eternal life, and I will raise him up at the last day."

The crowd started arguing among themselves. "We know his parents, Joseph and Mary. How can he now say, 'I came down from heaven?'"

Jesus interrupted, "Stop grumbling and listen." He continued, "I tell you the truth, he who believes has everlasting life. I am the bread of life. Your forefathers ate the manna in the desert, yet they died. But here is the bread that comes down from heaven, which a man may eat and not die. I am the living bread that came down from heaven. If anyone eats of this bread, he will live forever. This bread is my flesh, which I will give for the life of the world."

"I tell you the truth, unless you eat the flesh of the Son of Man and drink his blood, you have no life in you. Whoever eats my flesh and drinks my blood has eternal life, and I will raise him up at the last day. For my flesh is real food and my blood is real drink. Whoever eats my flesh and drinks my blood remains in me, and I in him."

When Jesus stopped teaching, you could have heard a jaw drop. This was difficult to understand and even more difficult to follow. The crowd had grown uncertain of what Jesus was talking about, but it was evident that there would be no more free meals. The show was over. I guess this bread was too hard to swallow. They turned and walked away. Notice that Jesus didn't chase after them, He wasn't about to force-feed them the bread from Heaven.

The crowds were interested in what Jesus would do for them rather than what they could become in Him. Jesus saw right through the disguise they didn't even know they were wearing. He looked at the people and saw their hearts. The people looked at Him and saw a man who could give them something for nothing. The crowd would have followed Jesus' trail of bread crumbs around the world, but when the free food ended so did their commitment. When their fancy was no longer tickled, they were no longer interested.

There is really little more than a few hundred years that separate many of us from the religious thrill-seekers of Jesus' day. Sometimes it's only what Jesus can do for us that keeps us loyal to Him. Does your faith and commitment boil down to what Jesus can do for you? Does your religious fervor hinge on whether the bread and fish keep coming your way?

How about it? You've bargained your faith away for trinkets, haven't you? You've looked Jesus in the face and asked what the next sign would be. Think about it. Trinkets take the place of faith when your love for Jesus depends on your feelings alone . . . when being healthy and wealthy is more important than being poor in spirit . . . when your attendance at the church relies on the quality of the day-care ministry rather than the quality of your spiritual life . . . when dessert socials grab your attention more than Bible studies . . . when you promise your allegiance to God if He will get you out of the particular mess you find yourself in that day.

We try to obtain a faith that costs us nothing only to get a bankrupt religion that costs us everything. Jesus tried to teach the crowd that day that the real prize was not in free bread but that true gain was a relationship of oneness with the source of spiritual bread, an eternal sustenance. The crowd didn't know that when it sat down to lunch, it was also sitting down to a lesson. In essence, Jesus was saying, "if you think this bread fills you up, then you've never really been hungry." Hunger for a life that is marked by a deep devotion to the Father and obedience even when the oven is cold and the basket is empty and the bread of this world is stale.

Don't follow Jesus because of what He can do but because of who He is and of who He makes us in Him. Jesus said, "Whoever eats my flesh and drinks my blood remains in me, and I in him." It is crucial that we ingest into our beings who Jesus is. The way He thinks . . . the way He acts . . . the way He loves. Everything about Him must become who we are. This is true communion with the Father.

After the crowd walked away from Jesus that day, He turned to His apostles and asked, "Are you going to leave me too?" Peter said it best and spoke for us all when he said, "Lord, to whom shall we go? You have the words of eternal life." Chase after trinkets and die of starvation. Follow the bread of life and never be hungry again.

Chapter Eight

Red-Faced and Red-Handed
John 8:1-11

*L*ittle babies are messy when they eat. This astounding fact may come as no particular revelation to you. Whether you're a parent or not, we've all seen little babies eat, or at least throw food around and eventually get some in their mouths. Birthday parties are the best. If you ever want your house redecorated with a cake and ice cream motif, just invite a little baby over for some birthday goodies. In an instant, little hands and little faces can become covered with icing and cake and ice cream and almost every other sticky substance known to man.

I love the scene of the little baby who, after quickly indulging in a forbidden snack, becomes covered with cake and ice cream. The mother enters the room and asks the child, "Did you eat the cake and ice cream I told you not to eat?"

With all the innocence and sincerity a two year old can muster, the baby replies, "No Mommy." Cute, huh? Sometimes, babies forget that cake doesn't become invisible when eaten or that sound still travels even when you're trying to be sneaky. Anyone who has ever seen a baby eat and play bounce the ball with little tomatoes, knows that it's easy for babies to get into some truly sticky situations.

Now, it's been a long time since I've eaten smashed birthday cake with ice cream covered fingers. It's been quite a while since I've stolen a cookie from the jar only to be caught red-handed. It's been a while since I was a baby. It probably has been for you too. Perhaps, however, it hasn't been so long since you felt as if you had cake all over your face while swearing up and down that you'd never touched it. Perhaps it hasn't been so long since you were caught red-handed rummaging through the cookie jar.

As I write this, I must admit I had one of those days today. I found myself red-faced not over what I had put into my mouth, but rather from what came out of it. I know you've been there before. You think no one is around, so you say some things you shouldn't. You think no one is watching, so you go ahead and take it. You're sure that everyone is gone, so you decide to live on the wild side. You are positive that what you're doing is absolutely secret, only to have the lights thrown on you like a surprise party and there you stand, red-faced and red-handed.

She had no excuse, no alibi. She was as guilty as the man who lay beside her. The first light of a new sunrise signaled them that their little secret had been kept safe for another night. The sounds of footsteps could be heard beginning to rustle about in the street. The smell of fresh bread filled the air. It was another morning of another day. She would go through this day, like many before, passing him by like a stranger on the street. All the while, they both felt so clever that their plan was working with such ease.

They were sure that their shadowed deeds would never be revealed. They had forgotten that sometimes sin is as obvious as birthday cake on the face of a baby. They were sure they were all alone, that their night together had been in secret. But on this morning, that would change. Perhaps it was through an angry wife or just some conniving teachers, but the word was out.

She heard a noise and turned in an instant to see a group of men barging into the bedroom. Some of them had stones in their hands. She could have denied her sin until she lost her breath, but the evidence was plain. They had seen it with their own eyes. Large hands grabbed her by the arms and began to drag her out into the street. The commotion had immediately drawn a crowd.

The morning sun was bright, so she covered her face with her hands and the bed sheet she had managed to grab through her rather quick exit. It could have been nighttime and she still would have hidden. The piercing stares and disdainful expressions of the people around her burned right into her soul. The men who grabbed her could have cared less about her affairs. They were using her to try to trap the Teacher. Their motives were impure, but then again her purity wasn't necessarily gleaming white either. She didn't even fight them. She knew what was supposed to happen next.

The men were making their way toward the temple, where a large crowd was gathered. She could hear the gasps and jeers of those who had already heard the news. She felt ashamed and alone and very afraid. She wondered where her accomplice in secrecy was. After all, the Law stated that both parties should be put to death. These men, though, had no interest in what the Law said. She was just their pawn, who happened to have been caught in the act.

Jesus stopped what He was saying as the attention of the crowd turned to the mob and the woman wrapped in bed sheets. They pulled her to the center of the crowd and stood her before the group. One of the men from the mob spoke up. "Teacher, this woman was caught in the act of adultery. In the

Law Moses commanded us to stone such women." He shouted. "What do you say?"

The men were using this woman and this question in hopes that they could trap Jesus. Meanwhile, the tears from her eyes rolled down her cheeks that glowed red with embarrassment. Regardless of what they had planned, she still had been discovered in her sin. She wondered how long they had known. She wondered if her liaisons had been so private after all. She wondered if her partner had set her up for this. She couldn't blame any of them, however, because she knew that she was guilty.

Just as a prisoner found by the spotlight while trying to escape, she could no longer hide what she had been doing. Just like a little child, she had forgotten that sometimes secret things are not so secret. Her thoughts raced as she waited for her punishment. A long period of silence brought her back to reality. She looked up and saw the Teacher bending down and writing something in the sand.

The men questioned Him again, demanding an answer. Jesus looked each one in the eyes and said, "If any one of you is without sin, let him be the first to throw a stone at her." Then He changed His gaze again to the ground and began to scribble in the dirt. What was He doing? Perhaps He was revising His sermon notes. Maybe He was trying to ignore the enraged stares of the Pharisees. Possibly, He was running His fingers through the dirt and recalling when, from that same soil, He had fashioned the first man, free from the terrible effects of sin.

Whatever may have been written on the ground in the temple courts that day has long since blown away, but what happened that morning in Jerusalem has been retold for centuries. The woman closed her eyes tightly in fear. One by one, she could hear stones dropping to the ground rather than hurling through the air. Finally, the air was still and silent. Everyone had gone and she began to be overwhelmed at how empty she felt.

For a moment she was alone with her conscience. Then, she heard the voice of the Teacher. He said, "Woman, where are they? Has no one condemned you?" She looked up to see for herself that all of her accusers had gone.

In a trembling voice she responded, "No one." She could hardly believe it. She certainly didn't deserve it. All of those who had dragged her into the temple were no where to be seen.

Jesus looked at her and said, "Then neither do I condemn you. Go now and leave your life of sin." The one against whom the offense had been the most serious, the one with the only right to judge evil because of His goodness was the same one who had set her free.

I don't know what the woman did after that day. I like to think that her encounter with the Master changed her life forever. I like to think that she no longer placed herself in compromising situations, that she was different as a result of her forgiveness. I like to think that, but I have no way of knowing whether it turned out that way or not. I don't know, because so many of us come face to face with Jesus and go away unchanged and unthankful.

We have all had situations of embarrassment, where we said or did something and were surprised to find we had been caught in the act. Perhaps, however, we still hope our deepest sins are shrouded in secrecy. We keep on returning to the same destructive habits time and again because we think that our disguise is thick enough to fool everyone, even God.

But all of us, you see, stand in the same place as the

woman. We don't know her name, but we feel as if we know her, because we can so easily identify with her life. We too stand in front of Jesus with nothing to say, no more excuses to offer, nothing left but our guilt and a stained conscience. Whether we are the ones who stand condemned or we are the ones trying to hide our sin by hurling stones at others, all of us stand imperfect before a perfect Redeemer.

We sometimes forget that the sin that we think is hidden the best is as obvious as cake smeared on our faces to the God who knows us so well. We are lonely and guilty just like the woman. But then it is Jesus who says to us, "It's all right. I don't condemn you. I forgive you. Now, go and don't sin like that anymore."

It has been a while since we have been babies. A few years have passed since we let our fingers dance through ice cream and a cake with a couple of candles on top. It has been a long time since we have felt so carefree . . . and so innocent. It is Jesus, however, who is there offering to make us new like that again. He offers to remove the guilt, to wipe us clean and to give us a second birth. Except this time, the celebration is not marked with cake and ice cream, but rather with the rejoicing of angels and the forgiveness of God.

Chapter Nine

20/20 Vision
John 9:1-41

A thousand sandaled feet shuffle through the streets. It's early morning, and the streets of the city are bouncing with people, moving chaotically at their own pace, in their own pattern. Each one has a mission. They have shopping to do, friends to visit, and work to get done.

Every morning the streets offer an array of captivating sights. The street vendors, with their colorful awnings and bountiful displays, have plenty of goods to look at and browse through . . . shimmering glass . . . rich, carved wood . . . beautiful bolts of material . . . shiny jewelry and stacks of useful pottery. Some even displayed their merchandise behind fencing. A perfect lamb can bring a good price, especially with the temple only three blocks away.

Now the temple was something to see. No building in all of Jerusalem could boast the majesty of the temple. It was breath taking. Yes, the senses are easily brought to life with a walk through the streets of Jerusalem. The smell of fish frying for breakfast fills the air. On your way to work, you can always count on hearing a few good jokes at the expense of the Roman Empire. You can also count on practically tripping over the beggars in the streets.

They clutter the walkways like litter. Most people ignore

them and keep walking. But occasionally someone will slow down just long enough to throw a few pennies in the direction of the more pitiful looking, who are pleading for help.

"Help a blind man?" was a phrase often heard throughout the day. Far more often than "Thank you for your generosity!" was ever heard. Especially from the man who always sits right at the corner, propped up against the wall of Stan's Bagel Shop. He's been here for years. Stan doesn't mind him sitting there. He even gives him the extra bagels that get burnt in the brick oven. The man has been blind from birth and it seems like he's been begging here since then. Every day finds him sitting, begging, and waiting for a generous spirit to happen by.

Days pass slowly for the beggar, today is Sabbath. It is a typical day. People still hurry by, it's just that they are on their way to temple, rather than racing to work. Afternoon rolls around and the streets are still crowded. Even some of the side streets have folks spread out telling stories and eating lunch. Jesus and His disciples emerge from the alley beside Stan's shop. Jesus had just left the presence of the Jews by way of another successful disappearing act. It's amazing how irate they become when you tell them you are Messiah, and that you have been around long before their "Father Abraham." Jesus had vanished from their presence not to avoid their questions, but to avoid the stones they were about to throw. It wasn't time for that, and it certainly wasn't the way things were planned.

As they round the corner, they see the blind man. He hears them approach and asks, "Good men, do you care to help a blind man?"

The disciples begin to ask the Master about the reason for this man's blindness. "Jesus, Is it from the sin of this man's parents or from his own sin that this man is blind?"

Jesus said, "It is neither this man, nor his parents' sin that has caused his blindness, but this happened so that the work of God might be displayed in his life." Jesus continued, "Listen, As long as it's day we must do the work of the Father. Night is coming soon, when you can get no work done. But, while I am in the world, I am the light of the world, and there's still plenty of light to see and work by."

After Jesus said that He bent down to the ground. The blind man repeated what he had said earlier, "Sirs, please help me, I've been blind from birth, won't you help a blind man."

One of the disciples started to reach into his pocket for a few coins, but Jesus had a lot more in mind than useless alms. Jesus was getting ready to supply an unexpected cure. Jesus spit into the dirt and made a mud paste. He took the blind man by the arms and raised him to his feet. Jesus then smeared the mud over the man's blind, bruised eyes. "Go," Jesus said, "Wash in the Pool of Siloam." The disciple put his handful of pennies back in his pocket.

The blind man took off for the Pool of Siloam, bumping into everyone and everything in his path. It must have taken a lot of faith to dart out into a crowded city street in search of a pool of water. He stumbled around until he finally made it to the pool.

He questions a passerby, "Sir is this the Pool of Siloam?" The man answered, "Yes it is, right in front of you." The blind man got down into the water and washed as Jesus had told him. As he brought the water to his face a second time, he clearly saw hands. His hands! He literally couldn't believe his eyes! He splashed in the water like a child on a hot day.

"I can see!" He shouted over and over, "I can see!" In all of his life, he never imagined the colors that now danced before him. He ran through the city soaking wet and still screaming. He marveled at what he saw. He saw things in such detail, like they were under a magnifying glass. He looked at the different faces of the people that stared at him like he had lost his mind, rather than gained his sight. He looked for Jesus, but He was no where to be found.

A crowd assembled around the man. They started arguing about whether he was the same man they had known to be blind. The man whose eyes were now opened looked like a new person. His face now held such life and eagerness. Funny how after you do what Jesus asks in faith, you get a new look about you, so new that you're hardly recognized.

"It's me!" He yells, "I'm the one who use to beg in front of Stan's."

"How do you now see us, as plainly as we see you?" The people asked.

"I met the one they call Jesus. He put mud on my eyes, and told me to go wash in Siloam. I did, and now I can see!"

The people took him to the Pharisees, who asked the man that was blind to explain everything in detail. The man did. The council didn't know what to make of the situation. Finally someone asked the man who had been healed. "What do you think about this Jesus fellow?"

"He's a prophet!" The seeing man replied. That didn't go over well at all. The council sent for the man's parents. When they arrived. The man ran to his parents and felt their faces, looking into their eyes. He studied their features. He told them, "Mother, Father, a man named Jesus gave me my sight, I can see!"

He clung to them, waiting for their reaction, as the Council guards escorted them before the Pharisees, but they gave no reaction. They were much too scared to make a big deal over their son's new gift of sight. Word had spread that anyone who gave this Jesus the time of day would be excommunicated from any sort of fellowship. This was especially true since that last confrontation that left the Pharisees throwing stones at a vanishing shadow.

The Council asked the two, "Are you this man's parents? Is this your son that was born blind? And, how do you suppose he can see all of the sudden?" The council waited in silence.

The parents answered, "Yes he is our son, and yes he was born blind," they couldn't deny that. "But as for how he can see, we don't know. He's a grown man. Ask him!"

The Council demanded that the man tell the truth before God, "We know this Jesus is a sinner . . ."

"Whether He is a sinner or not, I don't know," The man interrupted. "All I know is that I was blind, but now I can see perfectly! "

The Council was enraged, "Tell us what He did to you!"

"I have told you people over and over, why don't you listen to me? Why do you keep asking me this, are you Pharisees ready to become His disciples, too!"

"You're nothing but dirt from the very beginning, you are a sinner!" they yelled at him. "You're the follower of Jesus, not us! We are disciples of Moses! We know that God spoke to Moses! As for this lunatic, we don't even know where He comes from!"

"Now that is remarkable," the seeing man said, "You need to know where He comes from before you even acknowledge Him. All I need to know is that I can see! If this man were not from God He could do nothing. I think this Council could stand to have their eyes open a little wider!" With that, the Council jumped to their feet and fired one insult after another at the man. They threw him into the street.

Strange, isn't it? There were more blind people in the streets of Jerusalem that day than the beggar. The Pharisees' eyes were blinded with religion. The cataracts of legalism and faithlessness kept them from seeing the plain truth.

The man's parents were blind as well. They were blinded by fear. So much so, that they couldn't see the miracle that stared them in the face, even if that face belonged to their own son.

The beggar was now face down in the dirty street. By this time Jesus and the rest of the town had heard the commotion. Jesus found the man lying on the ground. He picked him up as He had before. Jesus asked him, "Do you believe in the Son of Man?"

The man asked, "Who is He, sir? point Him out to me so that I might believe in Him." Jesus said to him, "You're looking at Him with your own eyes. He is the one speaking to you right now. Don't you recognize My voice?"

"Oh, Master," the man said, "I believe in You!" And he worshiped Jesus. Now, the beggar turned believer saw with 20/20 vision.

Jesus looked to the Pharisees and to those gathered and said, "For judgment I have come into this world, so that the blind will see and those who see will become blind." The Pharisees standing nearby said, "I guess you're going to tell us we're blind now. Do we need some of your magic mud Jesus?" If truth had been a snake, it would have bit them. They never saw the truth, only a distorted image of what they believed to be true.

Jesus looked at them with God vision, and said, "If you were blind, you would not be guilty of sin, but I'm afraid that since you claim to see so well, your guilt and your blindness will stay with you!"

Can you see well enough to see yourself in the man who was blind? Do you notice anything similar between his condition and yours? Have you found your life consisting of one accident after another because of your blindness? We've all begged for help haven't we? We would have settled for the darkness but God had the light of never ending day in mind. We would have settled for a coin, but God had a cure.

With just enough faith to walk to the pool, we got up . . . still blind, still bumping thoughtlessly into the obstacles that stood in our way.

We washed in the pool beneath a fountain called Calvary. Then and there we received our sight. We don't know how. We don't know why. We can't explain it. We just know that, once we were blind, but now we can see!

Sin has a way of blinding us, doesn't it? It blinds us of who we really are and sends us to the streets, begging for a coin instead of a cure.

But hold on. Look out! When you come in contact with Jesus, prepare to be changed. When Jesus applies salve to your eyes, prepare to see as you never have before. When Jesus applies salve to your soul, prepare to be a display case full of God's power. God displayed His power in a powerless blind man. A man who couldn't help himself, but needed only to trust the power of a man named Jesus.

"And God raised us up with Christ and seated us with him in the heavenly realms in Christ Jesus, in order that in the coming ages he might show the incomparable riches of his grace, expressed in his kindness to us in Christ Jesus. For it is by grace you have been saved, through faith, and this not from yourselves; It is the gift of God—(Ephesians 2:6-8).

God has made us the recipients of the riches of Christ Jesus, and has displayed His power and mercy in us through giving us the gift of His grace: our sight. Sight to see ourselves for the blind beggars we are, and a faith strong enough to be the believing benefactors He has called us to be. hank God . . . I was blind, but now I see.

Chapter Ten

Broken Hearts and Empty Graves
John 11:1-44

*T*he halls of their house are empty tonight. Only a few sparse lights offer a dim glow where once every light was left on. Through her tears she ponders the irony of it all. Only a few nights before the hospital had felt just like this. Only a few lights broke the darkness of the corridors. Only the occasional wail of a siren shattered the eerie silence. Only her husband's hand on her shoulder reminded her that she was not in a nightmare.

Most of all, though, the loneliness was the same. The emptiness she felt now was a mirror reflection of the loneliness she felt that night in the hospital: the night her little boy died. He had been sick for a long time and they had taken him to every specialist they knew of, spent every last cent they had. Money was no object. Time and again, she and her husband had prayed for their little boy. They prayed night after night that God would heal him. They knew everything would be all right.

God was a very real part of their lives and their faith was strong. They felt confident that God listened to their prayers and that He would answer them. But now, they just weren't sure anymore. Where was God when they needed Him the most?

"If you had only been here God, if you had only done something, this never would have happened!" She wept, partly at how those words made her feel, but mostly at how lonely she felt at the loss of her son and at how angry she was with God. She had been faithful all of her life and this is how God repaid her. She had loved God and she thought God had loved her. Now things were so confused and so unsure.

She and her sister had been friends with the Lord for many years and had spoken with Him often. Many of their family gatherings had noted His attendance. He had become a very dear friend. These past few days however, they had longed for His presence but He was nowhere to be found.

The winds blew hot across the Mount of Olives and through the streets of Bethany. Mary sat beside the bed of her brother swabbing his sweat-drenched forehead with a cool damp cloth. She fought to keep the sleep out of her own eyes while she allowed a few moments slumber to her sister Martha. Hundreds of murmured prayers fell from her lips as she watched the health of Lazarus quickly deteriorate. They had sent word to Jesus, but every glance at the vacant horizon only lowered her hopes a little more. Where was He? Why hadn't He come?

Later that same night, the sisters watched as Lazarus struggled with every breath until he struggled no longer. Burning tears streamed down Mary's cheeks. It was not supposed to turn out this way. She knew that Jesus loved her and her sister, and that He loved Lazarus. Where was He when they needed Him the most? Where was God in the midst of their pain?

A genuine prayer becomes a burdensome memory when the answer you expect is not the answer you get. We know that God is love. The Bible tells us that. But what happens when God doesn't show that love in the way we want Him to? Since the first death outside of Eden through centuries of funerals, God has heard the question, "Why?" Why do bad things happen to good people? Why does life have to change? Why do people have to die? Why do I have to be left behind with a head and heart full of memories? Why don't you do something about this, God? Why didn't you answer my prayers? Why didn't you come a little sooner?

Four days had passed. Four days of weeping, wondering and waiting. Why had Jesus not come when they told Him Lazarus was sick? Where was Jesus when His friends needed Him the most?

Where is God when you are hurting? I'll let John tell you. In his Gospel he writes, "The sisters sent word to Jesus, 'Lord, the one you love is sick.' When he heard this, Jesus said, 'This sickness will not end in death. No, it is for God's glory so that God's Son may be glorified through it.' Jesus loved Martha and her sister and Lazarus. Yet when he heard that Lazarus was sick, he stayed where he was two more days."

That may sound a little strange to us, but it is Jesus in typical style. Where is Jesus when His friends need Him? Right where He always is . . . in control. Jesus knew what the outcome was going to be. He knew that in a few days He would exhibit His power and answer their prayers. Unlike Mary and Martha and you and me, Jesus can look into tomorrow to give us peace today.

But there is more than the confidence in His eyes that tells us about His love for His friends, there are also His tears. Martha had already spoken with the Lord and had returned to get her sister. Mary darted out of the room with a fury. Everyone thought emotion had overwhelmed her and she had returned to the tomb to cry once more over the body of her brother. Instead, she ran to meet Jesus.

Mary fell to her knees, sobbing. "Lord, if you had only been here, my brother would not have died." There is an unwritten rule that says when one person cries, everyone cries. Mary's renewed weeping beckoned more tears from the eyes of her friends.

Jesus could feel a lump forming in His throat. A chill raced down His spine. His eyes became glazed and His vision grew blurry with teardrops. He choked out, "Where have you laid him?" They led Him to the side of a small hill to a tomb that had been carved deep into a rock wall. The entrance had been closed with a large slab of stone.

Jesus' body started to quiver. He looked up to Heaven and a burning tear streamed down His cheek and into His beard. What was He doing? He was weeping. There was God in the flesh crying over the death of a dear friend. There was Jesus shedding the same bitter tears His friends had shed for the past four days. "Then the Jews said, 'See how he loved him!'"

Another voice from the crowd was not so sympathetic, the words were filled with hurt. "Could not he who opened the eyes of the blind man have kept this man from dying?"

But when the crying ceased, that was exactly what He intended to do. Even though He knew that in a few short moments, He would call Lazarus from the tomb, He still cried. Jesus not only knows the future but He knows the present. When His children hurt, He hurts. When we shed tears so does He. When the grave claims another temporary victory, He longs to clothe us with eternal victory. Regaining His composure, Jesus spoke again, "Take away the stone."

Martha stopped Him, "But Lord, by this time there is a bad odor, for he has been there four days." Martha remembered a crucial fact that had been impressed upon her several times before. After four days in the tomb, not much more can be done. But then again, Jesus was never noted for His funeral messages.

Broken Hearts and Empty Graves

Jesus reminded her, "Did I not tell you that if you believed, you would see the glory of God?" Several of the men from the crowd pushed the stone away from the entrance and Jesus began to pray. "Father, I thank you that you have heard me. I knew that you always hear me, but I said this for the benefit of the people standing here, that they may believe that you sent me."

Then, there was a moment of silence. The mourners grew quiet. And Jesus thundered, "Lazarus, come out!" Every breath was held and every eye was glued on the door of the tomb. Inside they saw something move. From the shadows walked Lazarus, living, breathing Lazarus, still wrapped in burial cloths.

The tears of mourning turned to tears of joy as bewildered friends gathered around the man they had watched die only a few days ago. The man who didn't have the strength to even move just days before was now sliding his feet through the dust, walking out of his own tomb! Jesus could be heard again over the noise of the crowd. "Take off the grave clothes and let him go."

Where is Jesus in the midst of our pain? He is right there with us. He is there removing the tattered grave clothes of fear and death and pain and setting us free; giving us new life and new hope found only in trusting Him.

Whether it be a bereaved mother and father, two crying sisters or even you, Jesus is right in the middle of whatever pain you face. For ,you see, Jesus was not only there at the open tomb of Lazarus, He was at His own open tomb. He was not only at the right hand of Lazarus, but is now at the right hand of the Father. He was not only there when they needed Him most, but He will also be there for you.

Now, do you see how much He loved him and how He cares for those He loves? Do you see how much He loves you? Death seems a little less permanent when you know the Giver of life. The grave is not such a terrifying place when you know that Christ has already been there. Tomorrow isn't quite so uncertain when you know that He didn't stay there, but rather looked death in the eye and arose victorious. Jesus not only said it to Mary, but He says it to all who have ever felt the sting of death, "I am the resurrection and the life."

Following the Right Shepherd

"I am the good shepherd. The good shepherd lays down his life for the sheep. The hired hand is not the shepherd who owns the sheep. So when he sees the wolf coming, he abandons the sheep and runs away. Then the wolf attacks the flock and scatters it. The man runs away because he is a hired hand and cares nothing for the sheep. "*I am the good shepherd; I know my sheep and my sheep know me—just as the Father knows me and I know the Father—and I lay down my life for the sheep.* I have other sheep that are not of this sheep pen. I must bring them also. They too will listen to my voice, and there shall be one flock and one shepherd. The reason my Father loves me is that I lay down my life—only to take it up again. No one takes it from me, but I lay it down of my own accord. I have authority to lay it down and authority to take it up again. This command I received from my Father" (John 10:11-18, emphasis added).

Chapter Eleven

All or Nothing
John 11:45-53

*T*here he sits, in the same high-backed chair he is in every Sunday. He sings along, though a little out of tune, with the choir behind him. A passing glance might mistake them for royalty, adorned in flowing robes of deep green, beige and gold, but they are not out of place. The preacher looks up from his hymnal to smile warmly to the audience, and as he looks beyond the sea of people his eyes wander across the magnificent tribute to God and to architecture erected here.

As they finish the last verse of "Calvary Covers It All," he looks out at the faces of the people in his congregation. The range of expressions is endless. Some smile. Some stare straight ahead. Some scan their bulletins for the next upcoming potluck. Some even stretch. Quite a few speak to the person beside them.

He spots Dr. Campbell a few rows from the front, every hair in place, his perfectly tailored suit, and a smile permanently plastered on his clean-shaven face. There goes Mrs. Jensen down the center aisle with her crying baby, or is it Ms. Hughes now? She and her husband divorced just last week.

God bless her heart, there's old Mrs. Ferguson resting her eyes again. That hymnal is bound to slip out of her hands any minute now. There, toward the back in the shadows, is Mr. Maxwell and his wife. If it's happening at the church, they'll be there.

He finishes his quick survey of the audience and glances down at his Bible. In just a few minutes, he will walk to the glass pulpit he has learned to love over the past few years and preach yet another sermon. He will tell the hungry listeners about God's love for them and how Christ died for sinners on Calvary. When he is finished they will all applaud and sing another song about Jesus and leave feeling a little better about themselves. But has the death of Christ made any real difference in their lives?

What bearing will the death of one man make on Dr. Campbell who sees death every day at the hospital? How will Ms. Hughes see Christ through her own lonely tears and those of her infant? What comfort will the cross bring to Mrs. Ferguson as she sits in her kitchen alone all day? What significance does a resurrected Lord really hold for the Maxwell's who spend so much of their time with His church? And what does the ultimate sacrifice mean to the preacher who talks and writes about Jesus every day?

He looks down again into his Bible. They were the same people who were responsible for the crucifixion. Their schemes paved the road to Calvary and nailed Jesus to the cross. It was because of them that the sacrifice had to be made. It was their idea that an innocent man had to die.

Busy travelers on the streets of Jerusalem carried a single message on their lips that day. The subject was not new. They had talked about Him several times before. Except today, the message was a bit more urgent for everyone. Many of them ran through the streets, pummeling through a barricade of people to tell the news . . . the news of what they had just seen in Bethany.

Some wanted to tell of a miracle. Some wanted to report a madman, but that is to be expected. Snatching a dead man back from the grave is no small matter, and it is definitely not neutral news.

The news from Bethany spread throughout the region like wildfire. The knocks came on his door one right after the other. He was greeted by a growing mob of very upset and uptight colleagues. The thought of having to deal with one more story about Jesus exhausted him, but he was the high priest and this was his job.

The temperature in the meeting room started to rise, partly because of their anger, mostly because of the hot air they were circulating. Seventy-one enraged men spoke loudly and dramatically to each other in little huddles. Caiaphas and seventy other equally enraged men spoke loudly and dramatically to each other in little huddles. Caiaphas loomed in the shadows speaking quietly to his friend Gamaliel. This Jesus had been stealing sheep from their fold for far too long. They could no longer remain disengaged. The time for action was now!

The meeting was called to order and the boisterous voices were dulled to a quiet. A man shouted from the back of the room, "We aren't accomplishing one thing!" Everyone turned to look. His white beard gleamed against his red face. One of his friends had been in Bethany at the funeral of Lazarus. He went there to mourn, not to be amazed! He went there to cry, not to be converted!

Voice after voice echoed a more angry and passionate plea for action. This was one issue that did not divide between partisan lines. Except for a very few who felt a growing acceptance of Jesus as Messiah, there was unity. "Here this man has the chutzpah to perform these miraculous signs. Who does He think He is, God?" There was a brief silence and a few raised eyebrows. "If we let this sort of thing go on, this healing and raising from the dead business, then everyone will believe in Him! Then the Romans will come and take away both our place and our nation."

The council voiced their approval. It's amazing how the scholarly leadership of Judea didn't recognize the terrific irony in their own words. Of course people would believe in Him, that's the natural response of a needy people to a welcome Messiah. But they couldn't even think about that now, there was a lot at stake here. Things like this might upset the Romans, who seemed to deserve more consideration than God anyway.

Caiaphas patiently listened to their grumblings, but he was too wearied to continue that much longer. He broke through the chatter of the men with a very bold voice. "You know nothing at all! You do not realize that it is better for you that one man die for the people than that the whole nation perish."

There it was. He knew what he had said broadly overstepped his authority. The Sanhedrin didn't have power to execute people, but no matter what had to happen, what strings had to be pulled, this man Jesus had to die . . . soon.

John says in his Gospel, "He did not say this on his own, but as high priest that year he prophesied that Jesus would die for the Jewish nation, and not only for that nation but also for the scattered children of God, to bring them together and make them one." The death of Jesus held great significance in the life of Caiaphas, but is that why Jesus had to die, to preserve a nation's identity and to keep seventy-one whitewashed sepulchres in power?

Caiaphas knew that the only answer to their problems was getting rid of it at the source. He was very proud to be a Jew and wanted to see the nation's heritage live on through upcoming generations, but he was also very fond of his position. He was one of the most respected men in the community and among his fellow council members. He was in authority of the government of Judea and held a great deal of political and religious clout far beyond.

If the Romans became unhappy with the way he and his associates ran the government there, then soldiers would come in and some Gentile governor would take over. Then all the power and prestige that had belonged to him and the council would be gone forever. There was only one possible solution: the Nazarene had to die! A few days later, that same spirit would prevail as the crowds persuaded Pilate to turn Jesus over to the Roman soldiers to be crucified. Caiaphas had gotten what he had wanted. Jesus did have to die. All of his wishes had come true, in more ways than one.

The death of Jesus held significance for Caiaphas, but the wrong significance. The murder of the innocent son of a carpenter meant nothing to Caiaphas, except that he could now be in control again. He saw nothing on the cross but a threat to his authority that had come to an end. The crucifixion was a mere symbol that he could cherish as a sign of his authority and use to his advantage.

The death of Christ meant a lot of things to a lot of people. To the zealots, it meant that no earthly kingdom would be established by someone as weak as this man. To the friends of Jesus, it meant the loss of their Messiah. To the afflicted, it meant their last chance at healing was gone. To the disciples, it meant a lack of guidance and purpose. To the Jewish leaders, it meant peace and harmony and fewer personal attacks. To Caiaphas it meant a sense of personal satisfaction.

Caiaphas thought all of his problems had ended, that his anger and frustration was over. Three days later however, the council would let another miracle pass them by. They had been angry at the healing of the blind man. They were furious that life had been restored to Lazarus. And now, they were incensed at the rumors that Jesus was missing from His tomb. The plan of God had passed right before their eyes, but their own plans had taken precedence.

The preacher looked up from his Bible. These are the same people for whom a Savior had to die. We are the ones for whom the cross was necessary. But even for people who claim to love God, the significance of what Jesus did there can become blurred and distorted.

Why did Jesus have to die? Yes, it was for you and me; but what significance does that death hold for us? Did Jesus have to die just so we can remain in control, or so we can feel a little better about ourselves? Was the sacrifice He made so we can remain in the limelight a little longer? Was the cross meant solely as an object to cherish or to have at our disposal so we can market ourselves a little better? Does the cross embody a symbol of status or salvation? Why did Jesus have to die?

What real difference will the message of the cross have made in the lives of people like Dr. Campbell, Ms. Hughes, Mrs. Ferguson, or the Maxwells? What difference has the message of the cross made in your life? What significance does it hold for you? Has it made any difference in who we are or how we act? Has it made any difference in the way we live? And is it continuing to make a difference by holding the proper significance in our lives?

Paul says in Romans 12, "Therefore I urge you brothers, in view of God's mercy, to offer your bodies as living sacrifices, holy and pleasing to God . . . ." How are we to respond to the ultimate sacrifice? Become sacrifices ourselves. Whatever significance we place in what Christ did on Calvary will show through in our lives. His sacrifice will show in our sacrifice.

Caiaphas could have had the riches of eternal life, but instead he settled for the poverty of temporary prestige. What happened on the cross was an amazing thing. Few events can stir the hearts of people 2,000 years after they occur, but the cross can and it does. If the cross holds little significance, then it holds no significance. Our lives are ultimately based on that fact. That is why one Man, Jesus Christ, had to die.

Chapter Twelve

Break the Bank
John 12:1-11

*B*illy's oversized piggy bank had sat in its own special spot on the floor, in the corner of his room, ever since his Mom and Dad brought him home from the hospital. The bank was a "welcome home" gift from his grandparents. They were the first to start a long tradition of putting money in Billy's piggy bank.

From that first day home, Billy's family and his parents' friends had emptied their pockets and put all their change, coin by coin, into his piggy bank. Quite a few bills had made their way into the bank too. Every year the bank got heavier and Billy got bigger.

When Billy was ten his huge piggy bank was so heavy, he couldn't even move it. It was at least three fourths full of pennies, nickels, dimes, quarters, and silver dollars. Coins weren't the only thing in Billy's bank either. There were ones, fives, tens, twenties, and there was even one fifty dollar bill from his eighth birthday when grandpa was feeling especially generous.

Billy loved to look through the slot down into the piggy bank. He tried to count everything he could see but he'd always loose track.

The older Billy got, the more reasons he found for smashing

the piggy bank open and cashing in on years of pocket change and cash.

When he was eight, he saw a toy that he had to have. When he was nine, all of Billy's friends had a new bike and he wanted one. Mom always said, "That money is going to be saved for something really important, something really meaningful." Billy didn't understand why that bike wasn't meaningful enough for Mom.

All the while, Mom and Dad insisted that half of Billy's allowance would go into the piggy bank. Now there were fewer coins and more bills making their way through the piggy bank slot.

When Billy was ten, it was a video game he wanted to break the bank for. When he was eleven it was $200 sneakers. At twelve, it was a CD player. At thirteen, it was a computer. At fifteen it was a computer upgrade.

Mom and Dad wouldn't budge. Billy dreamed of taking a hammer and smashing that stupid grin off the face of the pig that had eaten all his money!

Billy went through high school and the bank still lived on, eating money left and right. Billy's desire to break open the piggy bank was a constant topic of conversation. It had become the family joke. Dad was the worst. He would offer to sell Billy his sledge hammer for $1,000 and ask if he was willing to take a chance on making a profit.

Billy thought with college coming up, Mom and Dad would have no trouble letting him break open the bank, but they wouldn't hear of it. It was like that piggy bank had become the family mascot. By the time Billy left for college, he had to work really hard to squeeze a single dollar bill down into the bank. It was full!

It was during his senior year of college, on one of his visits home, that Billy sat down with his Mom and Dad. He began the announcement this way. "Mom, Dad, I've finally found a good enough reason to break open my old piggy bank."

"What's that, son?" They asked.

"Well, you know Beth and I have been dating for about two years now. She's the most important person in my life. I'm going to ask her to marry me. I have the ring picked out and some money saved up, but I'll have to break open the bank to have enough."

Billy's parents consented and the ceremony began . . . that is the ceremony of breaking the bank. Their family stood in a circle. Dad had a prayer for the pig. With one massive swing of Dad's sledge hammer Billy shattered that 22-year-old piggy bank. An avalanche of coins and bills came pouring out. Billy knelt down to pick them up. He had finally found something important enough, meaningful enough, to break the bank.

She knelt down at His feet. Those gathered around the supper table with Jesus just stared at her. She had no business interrupting their dinner! This was a meal in honor of Jesus and this sinful street woman was interrupting and offending the entire group.

But her eyes only focused on Jesus . . . she began to weep in His presence. Tears streamed down her face and fell to His feet. She wiped them with her hair. The disciples and the others gathered there, sighed with aggravation. Eyes rolled and smiles turned to scowls.

Then the woman unwrapped a bottle and rose to her feet. What's she doing? She took a moment and gazed at the bottle full of expensive perfume like she was bidding farewell to an old friend.

The perfume was expensive, a year's worth of wages. She had saved all her life for this and then the unexpected, the unrealistic, the unreasonable happened. The woman broke the bottle of costly perfume and poured it over Jesus. The strong but pleasant fragrance filled the room and so did the not-so-subtle discussion of the others.

"What a waste!" "That must have cost a fortune. How stupid. We are suppose to be good stewards of our wealth, not poor it out for nothing!"

Then Judas spoke up on behalf of the group. He pointed his finger at the woman and said, "Why wasn't this perfume sold and the money given to the poor? It was worth a year's wages!"

Judas may have seemed concerned about the poor but he was mostly concerned about his pocket. He was the treasurer and he helped himself to the money meant for things like helping the poor. Jesus saw right through his thin disguise.

"Leave her alone," Jesus said, "She did what she could. The poor you will always have with you . . . but you will not always have Me here."

What the disciples saw as waste, Jesus saw as worship. The unreasonable extravagance that didn't make sense to them, pleased Jesus. What they saw as misuse, Jesus saw as motivated from the heart.

Jesus saw worship. They saw waste. Jesus saw service, surrender, and sacrifice. They saw squander.

But who's right after all? Don't they have a point? We have enough demands on our pocketbook. Our money gets stretched to the limit. We've got a lot of financial responsibilities. Surely Jesus doesn't expect us to empty our bank accounts and sell our stuff? Isn't it enough if I put in my time in at church? Isn't it enough if I punch my spiritual time card? I put a few dollars in the plate every pay day. Isn't that good enough?

Sometimes that's really the way we feel about it. Shouldn't

that attitude bother us a little? It should bother us, because I think the people around the supper table that night probably shared that attitude. The problem is, Jesus covered in priceless perfume and the woman holding a broken bottle, are on the other side of the supper table and I think they had a different perspective.

But why the expensive perfume? Why so much? Couldn't the woman have just come in and spent time with Jesus? If she wanted to worship Jesus, she could have sung him a song or told Him how much she loved Him or baked Him some cookies.

But she didn't. I think she was so overcome with the desire to worship Christ, she was so consumed with showing her love, that it made perfect sense to grab the most priceless possession she had and present it to Jesus.

I'm sure she wasn't opposed to telling Jesus how much she loved Him. I'm sure she wasn't opposed to singing a song of praise in His honor. Maybe she was tired of just doing those things alone. Maybe there was something deep down that called her to sacrifice it all for God.

Take a moment and look around that candlelit room. Can you find yourself there? Are you like the woman who gave it all to Jesus? Are you the one who broke the bottle of costly perfume? Or are you among the group who was shocked at sacrifice?

Sacrifice shocks us, doesn't it? It's so uncommon today. Why would anyone, we wonder, be committed to the point of such sacrifice? That is unless they thought they owed everything to the one for whom they were sacrificing.

Were those at the table so upset at the woman because they were appalled at her so called " waste," or were they a little upset that they had been outdone. Remember, they were throwing Jesus a dinner in His honor. Suddenly that didn't look so extravagant in light of this street woman's costly sacrifice!

If we're honest with ourselves most of the time, we'd rather take Jesus to dinner than take our prized possessions off the shelf and lay them at His feet.

We'd rather sing Him a few songs than make ministry part of our budget. We'd rather just show up . . . than sacrifice.

Let me ask you a question. Have you broken the bank for Jesus lately?

We take out loans for houses, cars, education, appliances, computers, and furniture. What about taking out a loan to give a chunk of money to the church or a missionary to reach people for God. "You've gotta be kidding." "You're crazy." "I've never heard anything like that in my life." "What a waste."

Let's talk about waste. Let's talk about all the crazy things we spend our money on. Think of all the money we spend on things we don't need. When you consider most of us spend more money on eating out Saturday nights than we'd ever dream of giving to God, it should really make us think.

Billy wanted to break open his piggy bank but Mom and Dad insisted it would be saved for something really important, something really meaningful. Then one day Billy found a reason good enough to break the bank.

The woman that interrupted Jesus' dinner party had found a reason good enough to break the bottle of costly perfume. She had found something. She had found someone so important, so meaningful, that even the greatest sacrifice she had to make still didn't seem like enough.

Will you break the bank for Jesus? Will you give all you have? Will you give all you are? Will you surrender everything over to the Lord of your life?

Chapter Thirteen

The Standard of Service
John 13:1-17

*T*hey looked no different from any of the other people who walked through the crowded streets of the city that evening. The one thing that distinguished this group of men from the others was their huddled conversation. Thirteen of them, twelve followers and one leader . . . or is that up for grabs?

The twelve men took no time to observe the people around them or the sights of the city. They were too busy debating greatness. No, they didn't debate the greatness of their named Leader, or the greatness of the things He had said. Instead they argued about which of the twelve of them could be counted as number one. Who could claim the title of greatness?

Twelve men discussing who among them was greatest can create quite a scene. However, their raging tempers and raised voices were somehow contained under the blanketed chatter of the street vendors and bargaining shoppers. The streets of Jerusalem were even more crowded than usual and busier than most evenings. It was time for Passover.

No one in the crowd noticed the twelve. There was too much to do to notice, too many people to single out twelve men. But their Leader watched them closely. He wasn't leading them. He followed behind them at a short distance. It was hard to breathe up there in their little group, too much hot air. There was hardly enough room to walk with them. Their inflated egos and puffed, prideful attitudes occupied the extra space in the busy street, and part of the sidewalk too.

Do you see Jesus back there? He's listening, watching with an expressionless face. He had interrupted their arguing before, why not now? The debate of "who's the greatest" was not a new one for the disciples. Why didn't He just set them straight right then and there? Maybe He knew that their insignificant power play would soon be silenced. Maybe the Master Teacher was preparing for His greatest lesson yet.

Teacher Jesus moved around His pupils and quieted them. "This is the place," He said, as He pointed to a narrow rock staircase on the side of one of the buildings. Each one of the twelve made their way up the steps. They still volleyed muttered comments back and forth. They didn't think the Master heard them, but He heard every word.

All thirteen men squeezed into the small upper room: Twelve fighting, one focused. Twelve filled with rivalry; one filled with resolve. The room was plain, but what was about to happen in that tiny room over Jerusalem was more than ordinary. The evening sun peered through the windows like a nosey neighbor, casting a golden glow over the twelve apostles and Jesus reclining at a table as they prepared for Passover.

A hush swept across the room as Jesus began to speak. He reminded them of the Passover and what it meant. He spoke of the Passover lamb that was slain so the people could be saved from death. He talked about the blood of the lamb being shed and then painted on the door posts of the homes of the Israelites so many years ago. He rose from the table, and blessed the meal that was set before them. Passover had begun.

The Standard of Service

The subtle evening sun threw shadows across the faces of each of the men. A deeper shadow shrouded itself over the disciple called Judas. None of the others noticed, but perhaps Jesus saw the murky form of Satan dancing around Judas. Perhaps He could smell the stench of betrayal in the air. Satan prompted Judas's thoughts of handing over the Master. It was as if the Devil held the script of the moment, prompting Judas line by line. It was just hours away from curtain, and Judas never missed a cue.

After the meal was finished, Jesus prepared to teach His disciples some important lessons. He had no trouble remembering their arguments over who was the greatest among them. He was about to show them exactly who was greatest. He had said before, "The greatest among you is the one who serves." He knew that God had given Him all authority and that He had come from God, and was returning to God. Jesus knew where He was from and where He was going. He knew that the next few days would find Him fulfilling His mission on earth.

You would think that after several years of ministry, after several years of teaching the twelve, He would get tired of show and tell. Showing them by His example and telling them the secrets of the kingdom. But He wasn't finished, not by any stretch of the imagination.

What's He doing? Jesus gets up from the table. See Him walk to the other end of the room? He was getting ready to serve. If there were any one person on the face of the earth that was worthy of being served, it was Jesus Christ. But the Messiah got up from His seat, removed His outer robe, and wrapped a towel around His waist.

Where did He learn to serve like that? Maybe it was all those years growing up, helping Joseph in his carpentry shop. I'm sure He was sent many times to go find the hammer and nails. I'll bet there were several opportunities for Him to hold a board in place for His earthly father to saw.

He learned to serve from the years of ministering to countless people in the streets. From touching the lepers, from making the crippled walk, from restoring sight and faith and life. He learned to serve from the very beginning.

As He takes off His robe in the upper room, is He remembering taking off the shining glory and majesty that surrounded Him in the courts of Heaven? As He wraps the towel around His waist, is He remembering donning a frail human body? A body that gets tired and sick. A body that runs out of energy, and feels pain and sorrow. Is He remembering His descent to earth. His descent of service . . . ultimate service?

Jesus bends down and reaches for the basin by the door. He picks up a pitcher of water and pours it into the basin. Do you see Peter at the table? He's wiggling like a worm on a hook. "What's He doing?" Peter asks everyone, "What's He doing!?"

Jesus isn't distracted. He sets the water pitcher down and picks up the basin. Look over His shoulder into the basin. Do you see His reflection in the water. Look at that face. The image of God who made man is mirrored on the water in a wash basin, maybe in more ways than one.

The Savior doesn't move for a moment. He stares at His reflection. What's He thinking about? Is He thinking about the lesson of service and greatness He was about to teach His disciples? Or is He thinking about the life lesson He would soon teach on a wooden cross just a few hills over, on the outskirts of the city?

If this lesson taught with water and towel wouldn't get through to them, maybe the one taught with a cross and a few nails would. Look at the reflection. It's distorted now. It's distorted because the tears of the Master have fallen from His eyes into the basin below. Do you see the tears distort the reflection of the Man who "was" before the worlds were formed? Do you see the tears of the Man who looked into the very face of God and who has no reason to look away in shame? Do you see the determination in the eyes of the God who was sent to earth to love the unlovable, to serve those not worthy of service, to die for people who didn't deserve the sacrifice?

Jesus brings the wash basin to each disciple and, without a word, begins to wash their feet as a servant would. Imagine. God had put all things under His feet, and now He was washing theirs! The sent one of God, the Messiah, took the form of a servant. He was used to being a servant by now. But every act of service would be pale in comparison to the service He was about to render all mankind on a hill called Golgotha.

Jesus finally made His way to Peter and began to loosen Peter's sandals. "No way, Lord, You can't wash my feet!" Peter said. What was Peter afraid of? Why was he afraid of being served by Jesus? Was Jesus messing with the pecking order that Peter had established? Was Jesus messing up Peter's image of himself? I bet Peter wouldn't have minded it as much if Jesus would have washed everyone's feet but his. You see, if Jesus washes Peter's feet, then that means Peter moves down the latter of prestige. "Don't wash my feet Jesus, If You are washing my feet then that means I've got to do the same thing. That means I've got to serve someone else. I'm not ready for that Lord. After all I'm one of the twelve. I'm part of the "Savior's Secret Service." I'm your main man. I'm not a servant."

Have thoughts like that ever crossed your mind? Have you ever been so concerned with position that you forgot priority. So concerned with station that you misplaced service. Have you ever looked at the fellow worker that no one talks to? Have you reminded yourself that you don't have time to fool with people like that? Have you ever ignored a piece of trash on the sidewalk? Have you reminded yourself that it's not your job to pick up after people? Have you ever seen the person on the side of the road asking for food? Have you reminded yourself that it's the Government that takes care of useless, unproductive people like that? Have you ever noticed someone having a bad day? Their hands are full and their thoughts are cluttered. Have you reminded yourself that you shouldn't get involved? Then perhaps we should remind ourselves of the same facts that Jesus reminded Peter.

"Peter, if I do not wash your feet you have no part with Me and My kingdom." In other words, unless you get this Peter, you don't understand me at all. Unless you see the importance of being the servant I now model for you, then I've been wasting My time. But how did Peter answer? He said, "Lord, then wash my hands and my head too."

No Peter, you don't get it. You don't get it. This isn't about bathing the head, it's about bowing the knee. This isn't about hygiene, it's about holiness and humility. This isn't about soap, it's about service.

Peter sat stunned while Jesus served him. The Master returned to His place and asked them, "Do you understand what I just did here? You call Me your Teacher and your Lord, and you've done well in saying that. But take a lesson, if I, being your Lord and your Teacher have now washed your feet, then you should wash each other's feet. Serve one another. I have set an example for you to follow."

I can't help but wonder if some repentance took place in that small room in Jerusalem that night. Jesus continued to teach. The hour was approaching. One of the disciples had been missing for some time. I think he was gone to buy bread, or was bread being sold? The bread of life.

Jesus and His eleven sat a while longer around the table. Jesus told them about what was happening. He told them that

He was the vine and they would be the branches. He explained how the world would hate them, but they didn't care. Their lives had been molded by the Master . . . changed, revamped, renewed.

After prayer, Jesus and the disciples left the upper room and started walking. They passed through the valley called Kidron. On just the other side of the valley, was an olive grove, where they often met. This time Jesus was in front of the group. He led them. Funny, there weren't any discussions to be heard of who would be the greatest. Everybody knew that Jesus was the greatest. They all knew that any act of service they performed would be so small in comparison to His.

As they walked, Jesus thought of what had just happened, and about what was going to happen. I'm sure Jesus knew that a few hills over, Judas now led soldiers to the garden, but Jesus kept walking anyway. He knew that every step toward the garden was a step toward the cross.

Chapter Fourteen

Dream Home
John 13:31-14:7

*T*hey stood with their backs to the gravel road and held each other's hands. They had taken their shoes off to feel the soft green lawn underneath them. The lush carpet of grass stretched all the way back to the hill and the little creek that flowed at its base. Maria squeezed Bill's hand a little tighter and smiled, "I can't believe it, this is going to be ours. Back there around that grove of trees is where we should put it."

He smiled back and wrapped his arm tightly around her shoulder, "It's going to be great. This land is so beautiful." They had been married now for eight years this past June. God had blessed them with two little girls with the determination of their father and the compassion of their mother. "I can't wait to tell the kids that this land is finally ours," Maria said, her eyes filling with tears, "We've wanted this so much, finally we are going to have our dream home."

The house they were living in now wasn't all that bad. It was cool in the summer and warm in the winter. In the fall, they made homemade pies from the apples that fell from the tree in their front yard. They had done their best to make it a comfortable place, even if it was a little small. Every time they had to move out of each other's way to get into the kitchen, they would dream a little dream. "When we get our dream home," they'd say, "I think we should have a big kitchen with a really nice fridge. You know, the kind that has ice and water in the door."

This would always get them thinking and they would get lost for a moment bouncing ideas off each other. "Wouldn't it be nice to have everything just perfect. There could be a big deck out back and we could finally get the girls that swingset they want. We could have a bay window with lots of plants and space to put a big Christmas tree in the living room." Their minds would wander as they imagined what their dream home would be like.

Something would always pull them away. Today it was that screen door with no spring slamming shut behind one of the girls. Bill just kissed Maria on the cheek and they both longed a little more for the dream home that would one day be theirs.

After a few months of sawing and hammering and moving a lot of dirt, the house was finally ready. Now, it was time to say good-bye to the old house and say hello to their little slice of perfection. But first came the awful task of moving.

The family had already started putting things away in boxes. They found it hard to believe that so much junk had accumulated over the past few years. Both Bill and Maria were pack rats and their "maybe" pile was getting bigger all the time. In a way it was kind of sad. The faded memories of all the good times they had here came rushing back to their thoughts. That night would be the last they would spend inside these walls that had become known as home to them.

All the dishes were packed, so breakfast was promptly served on paper plates. Nobody ate much, because they were so excited to get the rest of their stuff into the new house. Maria cried when they pulled out of the driveway. But a few miles away, her tears quickly dried as they pulled off the gravel onto the blacktop in front of their new home. They had been to the house many times during its construction. This time, however, was official. This was now their home and it was everything they had ever dreamed of.

Bill and Maria had taken a week off work so they could enjoy their new place. None of it hardly seemed real. Their dreams had finally come true. In the weeks that followed, they loved waking up in their new bedroom and taking strolls in their new neighborhood.

But you know what, after a while, even a dream home can have its problems.

Dream floors can become messy. Dream pipes can become clogged. Dream bulbs can blow. Dream closets can become cluttered. Dream fridges can go on the fritz. Dream screen doors can slam too loudly. Sure, Bill and Maria still treasured their new home. But even treasures can become corrupted with moths and rust.

What makes a good dream home anyway? The very name would suggest that it's a place that satisfies great wishes and deep longings. A place that only the imagination can truly comprehend. For Bill and Maria, a dream home meant more space, beautiful scenery, only the best appliances and furniture and a good place to raise their children. For you, a dream home may mean something different. Maybe it's moving somewhere close to your dearest friends, a log cabin back in the woods, somewhere with peace and quiet, a palatial estate or even just a place that is easier on your pocket book. I really can't begin to describe your dream home, because it is a place usually beyond description. A fond place we love to visit in our minds when the real world closes in around us.

When life gets tough and bills pile up and frustrations keep us awake at night, we love to imagine that pristine place where the world is new again. Dream homes seem even more perfect when where we are is far less than perfect. This was the case for the group of friends and colleagues as they sat and ate together. One of them had already decided to cash in his dreams for a handful of nothing. The others listened intently as their friend and mentor spoke, "I will only be with you a little longer, but where I am going you cannot yet come. So then, it is important that you love one another all the more."

The men could not believe what they were hearing. Why couldn't they go with Him. It certainly wasn't because of their resolve. One of them, named Peter, stood up and said, "Why can't I follow you now. I will lay down my life for you."

The Master spoke back to him, "I'm afraid that's just not true. As much as you think that, I know that even before the night is overyou will deny that you even know Me." Nothing destroys the notion of a dream home like painful reality. Peter thought that his life was at its peak. He would have done anything for Jesus. But brick by brick, his life came crashing down around him. It was then that Jesus reminded him to think about his dream home.

"Do not let your hearts be troubled," He said. "In my Father's house are many rooms; if it were not so, I would have told you. I am going there to prepare a place for you. I will come back and take you to be with me that you also may be where I am." Your dream home, My friends, is under construction.

We try to imagine a dream home, a place where everything is perfect. We long for a place where life is simple and love is not hindered. Our spirits ache for a place where worries cannot go and tears are not necessary. We desire to take up residence in a safe place where our best friends are with us and our troubles are a million miles away. We not only want, but we need a dream home.

Dream Home

The only problem is that we think that dream homes can be made using wood and nails and carpet and glass. We think that the right piece of land in a good neighborhood and all the best furnishings can make us as happy as we imagine they can. But soon we learn that no matter how grand our residence, it can never truly be perfect.

The next time your mind wanders away to a magical tour of your dream home, take a look out the window. I think you'll discover if you really look hard enough that you are no longer on earth. There is no place here that can create that kind of joy or happiness. When we long for our dream home, what we are really longing for is a Heavenly home, an eternal home.

Jesus is already preparing it for us. And He was good enough to let us to catch a glimpse of it in our hearts. He said one last thing to His disciples in that upper room, "You know the way to the place where I am going." He not only teases us with glossy real estate photos, He makes our estate real, and even provides us with a road map to follow. Thomas asked what you may be asking, "How do we get there?" Jesus' response to him is His response to us, "I am the way and the truth and the life. No one comes to the Father except through Me." Your dream home is more than a dream, it is a promise, and it is closer than you think.

Chapter Fifteen

Plugged In
John 15:1-8

*I*t has happened to most of us at least once. You're ready for a nice, leisurely evening in front of the television. You've fixed yourself a snack and snuggled down into your favorite easy chair. You reach for the remote control. As your fingers stretch to press the "power" button, you fill with anticipation and then . . . nothing!

What could have happened to the television? It was working last night. What could possibly be wrong? You launch from your easy chair in a huff, stomp over to the TV and begin to pound on the top and sides. "What's wrong with you, you piece of junk? My favorite show is about to come on, and all you can do is just sit there!" After a while, you realize that all the pounding and persuasive talking in the world just isn't going to fix whatever could be wrong with your set.

The next morning, you call the repair man and meet him at the door that afternoon. You leave him in the living room with the television and in moments he says, "Everything's fixed."

"Fixed? So soon?" you ask. "What was the problem?"

"Pretty simple to take care of," the repairman replies. "It seems that your set has experienced a difficulty in the transference of power. In layman's terms, your set was unplugged."

"Unplugged!" Then you remember vacuuming behind the

television just yesterday. That must have been when it happened. "Well, it looks like I missed my favorite show and spent the night in silence for nothing."

"No charge today," the repairman adds as he walks out the front door, trying to contain his amusement.

It doesn't take a technological genius to know that no matter how well things are working inside your television, it's not going to work if it's not plugged in. You can have the most expensive TV on the block. Your set can have a thousand different fancy features, but if the plug doesn't connect with the power source, all you have is a box of wires and gizmos.

Without the power from the wall outlet, your TV won't produce the results you desire. It won't, it can't, do a thing. If it isn't plugged in, it's not worth much at all.

Jesus said, "I am the outlet." No, that's not a direct quote, but it might as well be. The message Jesus spoke is the same. Read some of the messages in Jesus' own words. "I am the vine you are the branches. If a man remains in me and I in him, he will bear much fruit; apart from me you can do nothing." Would you stop for a moment and really concentrate on that last statement. Let it sink in. "Apart from me, you can do nothing."

Don't you think Jesus is taking this a bit too far? Maybe you're saying to yourself, "I've seen people who weren't always 'plugged in' to Jesus who have done some spiritually significant things." Really? Are you sure? Have you ever known someone who looked very spiritual on the outside but really was not?

If you are like most of us, you can find the most vivid example of spiritual mask-wearing by looking in the mirror. There have been times in our lives when we weren't close to

God. We neglected time with Him. We weren't hungry for His Word. We really didn't care that prayer had lost its priority in our lives. Yet, we continued wearing a false face of spirituality.

If you're a pro at looking spiritual, not even the people closest to you can always see the "real you" behind the mask. In fact, you can even convince yourself that the spiritual image you convey is a true reflection of who you are. When in reality, you are empty and powerless.

Now is it a little easier to believe that someone can seem spiritually productive and healthy, and all the while not be "plugged in" to God? The truth is, it's sometimes difficult to decide what is truly productive in the spiritual world. A church may be doing well, but because the minister wasn't plugged into the source of power, his ministry will eventually stop bearing fruit and die. A friend may seem to be leading a complete Christian life and then suddenly you hear the news. Her marriage is ending. She was unfaithful.

The severed branches might take a while too look dead, but they started dying the moment they were cut off from the life-giving vine. The television might look fine just sitting there in your living room, but when you put it to the real test and push the "power" button, nothing happens if it's not plugged in. And you might look fine just sitting there in the pew, but when you are put to the real spiritual "tests" in life . . . when you go to push the "power" button . . . nothing happens.

Jesus said, "Apart from me you can do nothing." Even if we completely accept that statement, the fact still often throws us for a loop. We are faced with a challenge in our spiritual lives and wonder why things don't work out. We can't conquer a particular sin we struggle with, and wonder why we can't move on. We scratch our heads and wonder why we aren't growing in our walk with Christ.

Maybe our cord isn't plugged into the outlet. Maybe we aren't realizing who the true power source is. Could it be that we try to accomplish great ministries and grand schemes for God without inviting Him to be part of the process? Could it be that we try to overcome sins with our resourcefulness and strength? Could it be that we try to move ahead spiritually by using unspiritual means? When we aren't tapped into the power source, is it any wonder we don't get powerful results?

Jesus is our source for life and nutrients and power and strength. Without Him, life is like a tree without a trunk, a car without a fuel line, an appliance without a cord, branches without a vine, people without power.

So if you want to miss your favorite show and spend the night in silence, don't plug the television into the outlet. If you want to miss a full life in Christ and spend your days and nights, maybe even eternity without Him, don't read His Word. Don't spend time talking to Him in prayer. Don't act on your faith and by all means don't plug into the power source, Jesus Christ! Because apart from Him . . . You can do nothing!

Following the Right Savior

"In a little while you will see me no more, and then after a little while you will see me. . . . I tell you the truth, you will weep and mourn while the world rejoices. You will grieve, but your grief will turn to joy. A woman giving birth to a child has pain because her time has come; but when her baby is born she forgets the anguish because of her joy that a child is born into the world. So with you: *Now is your time of grief, but I will see you again and you will rejoice, and no one will take away your joy* (John 16:16-22, emphasis added).

"My prayer is not for them alone. I pray also for those who will believe in me through their message, that all of them may be one, Father, just as you are in me and I am in you. May they also be in us so that the world may believe that you have sent me. I have given them the glory that you gave me, that they may be one as we are one: I in them and you in me. May they be brought to complete unity to let the world know that you sent me and have loved them even as you have loved me. *"Father, I want those you have given me to be with me where I am, and to see my glory, the glory you have given me because you loved me before the creation of the world"* (John 17:20-24, emphasis added).

Chapter Sixteen

Freed for Friendship
John 15:9-17

*B*right rays of sunshine pour across the huge white columns and through the windows of the big Georgia mansion. Long shadows are cast upon the wall just hiding a calendar marked 1856. The hot summer winds blow across the fields of cotton and across the leathered backs and faces of Negro men and women who work those fields. Their backs stream with sweat from the heat but don't bear the marks of a whip as do the backs of some of their friends.

The faint glimmer of hope shines in their eyes rather than the dull cloudiness of anguish, for their master has always been a just man who has treated them like human beings instead of cattle. They have seen many suns rise and set on the plantation. They have spent many hours working harder than most men would ever dream.

However, they have not only spent time in the fields but also at the master's table, inside the big house, inside the master's care. He gives them plenty of food, a decent place to rest, and a sense that he sees them as more than just slaves.

It was not too many years ago, eleven to be exact, that the master and his wife had their first child, a son. The compassion they had shown toward their workers was great, but it was nothing compared to the love they lavished on their little boy. From the moment he was born, he was taught what it was to love and he learned how to treat others the way he wanted to be treated.

As he grew up, he not only knew the love of his parents but also of the slave women who cared for him. He knew not only the love and acceptance from people he called Mom and Dad, but he knew love from those he called friends: the plantation workers and their children. They could often be seen running through the fields, skipping stones across the pond in front of the mansion, or wading barefoot in the cool waters that flowed in the little stream over the hill.

Every summer day was a special event, every nightfall a blessing, every month and year a milestone. However, each year of his young life saw more and more responsibility laid on his shoulders. His father placed him in charge of more of the family's business and gave him increased authority over the slaves.

One of the drawbacks of growing up is that you begin to realize that the world is not perfect. By the time he was sixteen, reality had set in to stay. In January, his state had seceded from the Union. In April, tempers heated up along with the weather in South Carolina and the first shots were fired at Fort Sumter. In the summer, he was left completely in charge of the household when his father joined men of like mind on the battlefields.

The fields at home in Georgia now belonged to him. Seasons passed with occasional letters from his father, but they soon stopped until the final letter came bearing the news that his father had been killed in battle. He was now the sole heir of the estate and its livelihood would now depend on him.

The end of the war not only brought peace to a ravaged country, but also freedom for the slaves. The servants on this plantation had never really considered themselves in bondage but freedom was always attractive. Remembering the love they had shown to him, he gave them a choice: to go or to stay on as hired hands.

Some of them left, but most remained and a select few of them became his partners in running the family business and taking care of the plantation. In his youth, they had been his companions, his playmates, even his mentors. When he was placed in authority over them, he did not forget that. Now, he no longer called them servants, but instead called them friends.

Their faces wore the image of discouragement. Everything about their lives echoed the fact that they were in slavery. Their efforts never seemed to be met with satisfaction, but rather with word that their master only desired more of them.

They knew that their master was just; that had been passed down through generations in their families. Over time, however, the increasingly heavy load that they carried on their backs had worn them down. Their burden had made them weary and their yolk had grown very heavy.

Their feet had trudged through the thick mud in Egypt. Their hands had made bricks to build monuments to the one who held them in bondage. They were in a strange land, laboring for a strange, foreign people who worshiped strange, unknown gods. Even later, against the backdrop of the lush gardens of Babylon, rattling chains and clanging shackles of slavery could still be heard.

It had been so long since they had last heard from their master, around 400 years in fact, but their master could no longer be silent because He wanted to be more than just their master, He wanted to be their friend. Eighteen hundred years before any Negro man worked in the fields of Georgia, a Man from Nazareth shared the wonderful news of freedom with His friends.

> "As the Father has loved me, so have I loved you. Now remain in my love. If you obey my commands, you will remain in my love, just as I have obeyed my Father's commands and remain in his love. I have told you this so that my joy may be in you and that your joy may be complete. My command is this: Love each other as I have loved you." "Greater love has no one than this, that he lay down his life for his friends. You are my friends if you do what I command. I no longer call you servants, because a servant does not know his master's business. Instead I have called you friends, for everything that I learned from my Father I have made known to you. You did not choose me, but I have chosen you to go and bear fruit—fruit that will last."

Imagine how the sound of those words rang in their ears. The master could sense their hearts beating a little faster. He could feel an excitement in the air. He could see the burdened, bloodshot eyes turn to Him as He spoke those words of emancipation to the heavy hearts of His hearers.

For generation upon generation, their people had been slaves of their religion. If they had not been slaves to God, then they had most certainly become slaves of the Pharisees and the Law. These were simple people who wanted desperately to serve God, but often felt powerless to do so. There were so many minute details to follow, so many miniscule points and subpoints to remember. It was like being in a labyrinth where one wrong move would send you meandering down the wrong path.

They felt trapped. They even felt like slaves, but they knew what lay on the other side. Maybe it's better to be a slave of one's religion than a slave to sin. Yet, they longed for something better. They longed for intimacy with God. They longed for a real living faith. They longed to come into God's presence and to be called "friends."

How often have you felt like that? How often have you longed for a faith that goes beyond words on a page? Longed for a relationship to a living God rather than an obligation to an object of conversation? Oh, we know all the things that are expected of us, like a good slave should.

We know that we need to read some from our Bibles. We know that we need to pray in public sometimes so people will think we have everything in order. We know just when to close our eyes in worship, just when to give a scolding scowl to the "sinner." We know how little we can do and how much we can get away with and still feel comfortable wearing the name "Christian." We know how to be good slaves, but not necessarily how to be good servants, or good friends.

Even as a friend, certain things are expected of us. Jesus said that we did not choose Him, but that He chose us to bear fruit. God has been stretching out His arms to His people for generations waiting to embrace them while they stared straight ahead, walked by Him and shallowly offered their sacrifices and mouthed empty words of prayer.

How many times have we passed up friendship only to settle for slavery? It's not that we don't know the Master's business, because He's shared all the ins and outs with us. It's not that we serve an unjust tyrant because His one command is that we love each other the same way He has loved us. It's not that we lack the opportunities of friendship, because He has shown the greatest act of friendship by laying down His life for us.

The apostle Paul says, "At one time we too were foolish, disobedient, deceived and enslaved by all kinds of passions and pleasures. We lived in malice and envy, being hated and hating one another. But when the kindness and love of God our Savior appeared, he saved us, not because of righteous things we had done, but because of his mercy" (Titus 3:3-5).

Cultivate your friendship with God today. Approach your friendship with Him like you would with any other person. Spend time with Him and get to know Him. Learn to develop a desire to know His heart. Listen for His voice and cherish His friendship with you. Don't allow sin to build a wall between you. Remember, at one time we were slaves, but because of Jesus Christ, we can now be called friends.

Chapter Seventeen

Truth on Trial
John 18:28-40

*I*n courtrooms across America today, gavels will pound and echo in the hearts of men and women, passing judgment from case to case. Lawyers will quibble and quarrel over pieces of evidence. The people with the black robes and the whole world draped across their backs will ponder the evidence and make their decisions. Sentences will be pronounced. Fines will be levied. Pleas will be made. Justice, hopefully, will be served.

Some will walk away with smiles, a victory finally won. Others will walk away in tears, a life utterly destroyed. Somehow through it all, the scales of justice seem to remain relatively balanced awaiting the next case to get its hearing. In courtrooms across America today, juries will listen intently, attorneys will argue eloquently, and judges will weigh carefully all of the evidence . . . facts and figures and testimonies that are all attempting to point to the star of the entire proceeding . . . the truth.

Perhaps there is nothing so important, yet so elusive as what we call the truth. The quest for truth is the single quest that consumes every one of us. Its effects go far beyond the wooden walls and plush carpets of the courtroom. The burning desire after the truth invades every part of our lives and demands that each of us look to find it.

Truth makes its presence well known in our relationships, in our homes, in our work places, in our schools, in our hearts, in every part of our lives. Truth is a very difficult thing to find and to hold, but the single thing that leaves the greatest void in us when it is absent. Truth is the most elusive personal trait to maintain but the thing we demand most out of others.

Truth demands complete allegiance. Perhaps that is why so many of us fail to find it, because life is often simpler without it. Truth pervades every aspect of our existence, but when all is said and done, it is ultimate truth that we need the most. What is ultimately true about our existence. What are the solid facts about who we are? Why are we here and why there have to be certain laws and rules that govern us?

Could it be that truth is something that is different for each of us? If that were so, then truth would lose that which makes it so special. We already have a word in the English language about personal "truth" that is subject to change. That word is called an "opinion." No, what makes truth unique is that it demands the same response from all of us. Truth is not a chameleon, it does not change its form to fit the opinion of the seeker. Rather, the seeker of truth must change himself in order satisfy what truth demands.

In court cases, only one decision is rendered. Truth is so unique that it stands distinct from all inferior opinions. When we arrive at the truth, it cannot then change but can only be accepted or denied.

Throughout the years, mankind has trusted the judicial process to uncover truth in matters where it is disputed. In recent times in America, court cases are more prevalent than ever as people take television's advice and "take 'em to court." Yet in the midst of all the cases that have been presented, there stand a select few whose decisions have affected much more than the litigants, but have changed the perception of truth itself for entire generations.

Our modern lives have been affected in some way by the decisions that were produced in a once modern-day court of law. These landmark cases have decided more than the issue at hand, they have also decided the course of history that would follow. History contains one particular case that came before an unsuspecting judge whose decision would change the life course of millions.

The soft light of the dawning sun cast its first shadows across the halls of the Praetorium. The governor's residence was dark and cool; his bed was soft and warm and quite frankly he would have much preferred the latter. This day however, his duties began earlier and more urgently than usual.

It seemed that a group of men had been up all night with a man they had been after for some time. Pilate didn't understand it all, but he at least knew that it had something to do with their religious customs, which he didn't care to put up with this early. To make matters worse, they refused to come to him. It would defile them you see. They couldn't possibly afford to look removed from God on such a special day, even though their hearts contained nothing of what God was really doing that made the day more significant than ever.

So Pilate came out to them to see what a great criminal they had brought before him at such an early hour. As he approached them, he saw the Man who was the fuel for so many rumors. The redness of His eyes gave away His tears and lack of sleep and the bruise on His body told that it had obviously been a long night.

Pilate was the first to speak, "What is it that you are accusing this man of?" This was probably more of a rhetorical question, but he was curious for what they had to say.

One of them loudly spoke up, "If this man wasn't a criminal, we would most certainly not be wasting your time, Governor." They really had no answer to give him, because the charge itself had lost its importance. They simply wanted to get rid of Him as quickly as possible.

In spite of the chilly air of the morning, they still wore a rather thin disguise, which Pilate, even in the dim light, could see right through. "Take Him yourself," Pilate said flatly, "Judge Him according to your laws and customs."

This forced them to come right to the point, "Well, we are not permitted to put anyone to death," they said. They were not interested in arriving at justice or arriving at the truth. All that consumed them was that this man had to be put to death. It didn't matter whether He was right or wrong, whether He deserved to die or not. To them, He had to die, it didn't matter why or how.

Pilate returned to the Praetorium and took Jesus with him, so that he could question Him without the senseless chatter of the Sanhedrin members getting in the way. Pilate didn't waste any time, "Are you the King of the Jews or are you not?"

Instead of a reply to the question, the condemned Man put the judge on trial and asked a question of his own, "Are you saying this on your own or did someone else inform you about Me?"

Pilate reminded the ragged Man standing before him that it was the Jews themselves and moreover their leaders who dragged Him into this court. The Man reminded him that if He were a king, then the kingdom must surely be different from any established on this earth, because the subjects were not fighting to keep Him out of the hands of the Jews.

The Man responded to Pilate by letting him know that he was standing before a king, but that the kingdom He represented was like no other Pilate had ever known. Even the very way the Chief Priests were having Jesus tried in a Gentile court and eventually the way He would die at their hands was not an accidental roadblock that interrupted His kingdom, but the one thing that this king had come to earth to do. The kingdom would not end but rather begin in these moments.

This kingdom was different, its king was completely unique. Jesus told Pilate that He came into the world to bear witness to the truth. In fact, the truth is the one trait that marks the followers of this kingdom. All who are of the truth hear the voice, the commands, of the king.

The question that Pilate asks next is really quite a logical one, especially for someone who is not a subject of the King of truth and thus cannot fully understand truth in its entirety. Pilate asks, "What is truth?" This trial was different from all before it or since because no singular aspect of truth was being debated, but rather truth *itself*, truth *Himself*, was being put on trial.

There was no social issue in debate. There were no ideas being hammered out. There was no little truth trying to be reached in a single matter. There was, however, the embodiment and the creator of our very idea of truth being questioned by a mortal man. Pilate got to ask Jesus face to face what truth was, never realizing he was staring directly into the eyes of everything that truth is.

However, in all the courtrooms of our hearts, where does that leave folks like you and I, who wage battles of trying to achieve personal truth in our lives every day. On a regular basis we weigh truth against our desires on a very precariously balanced scale. Often, we will weight the end that contains our meager desires because we, like the Sanhedrin, lose sight of what really is important. We are as guilty as they were of achieving what we want at any cost, never giving truth a second thought.

Our world is full of people who are trying to figure out what truth is. The streets team with myriads of endless faces and empty hearts trying to find the light of truth in the thick fog of clashing ideas, desires, and loud voices. Perhaps one of those faces looks just like your own and one of those hearts aches exactly like yours.

So then, what is the answer to the question, "What is truth?" The answer is really quite simple, accepting it and living with it is what becomes difficult. Jesus said, "I am the way, and the truth and the life. No man comes to the Father except through Me." The truth is not a set of facts or figures put in the proper order. The truth is not a set of values that differs from person to person. The truth is a man; a Man who was really God in disguise.

When we say that we want to find the truth in certain matters, all we are really doing is listening for the voice of Truth Himself. Jesus told Pilate, "Everyone who is of the truth hears My voice." It is impossible for us to fully comprehend truth if we do not understand it in full obedience to Christ, the one who created truth and is truth.

If we want to find truth, we find the Man. He is easy to find. He has told us where He is, at the right hand of the Father in Heaven. All we have to do is seek after Him and not only will we find the Truth, but the Way and the Life as well. For those of us who have already found the Truth but for some reason still have trouble knowing what is right and what is wrong, let us take a moment to be still and listen for His voice. Everyone who is of the Truth hears His voice, and if you listen very closely, you will hear His voice calling your name.

Chapter Eighteen

The Udeserved Inheritance
John 19:1-42

You've just gotten your "reality check" in the mail . . . it's Monday. The relaxation of the weekend is behind you now, and a long week of the "same ol's" greets you with the buzzing of the alarm clock. You know what we're talking about. The same ol' drive to work. The same ol' grueling routine of your thankless job. The same ol' punching your card and wanting to punch your boss.

But you can't really blame Monday. It's the same story with any day that ends in "y." You take the same ol' drive home. Today, though, you get the distinct pleasure of stopping by the market. The usual bread, meat, and toilet paper find their way into your cart. You toss in some Calgon, wishing it really would take you away. As much as you would like to take a nap in the produce section, you know there's a lot waiting for you at home.

There should be a gold medal for balancing a fist full of mail in one hand and a bag full of groceries in the other while tripping over the tenacious dog and dodging past a family starved for supper and attention. But there's not. You don't even pick up the bronze. Instead your reward is having to sit down at the table and sort through the stack of mail that urgently awaits.

Follow Me Again

You look. "Bill . . . bill . . . bill . . . oh look honey, we may have just won a million dollars! Wouldn't that be our fourth this month?"

Wait a minute. What's that? It's addressed to you, but you don't recognize the handwriting. You break the seal of the envelope. "Do we know anyone from England? We don't know anyone from England."

You unfold the letter and begin to read. This can't be for real. You continue reading. For real or not, your stomach fills with an unsettling excitement.

You chuckle and begin to read aloud. "We regret to inform you of the passing of . . ." You scratch your head, you've never heard of him before. You've never heard anyone mention a great, great uncle . . . "On behalf of his household, your presence is requested at the final reading of his last will and testament. At that time, the sum of his ninety-million-dollar estate will be divided among his seven living relatives. As an heir to the inheritance your presence is of utmost importance. Plane tickets and a map are enclosed."

Sounds pretty fantastic, doesn't it? Don't say you've never dreamed it would happen. We have all had those moments, when at the height of mediocrity, we've wished that someone would hand us an undeserved inheritance.

We have all played out that unbelievable story in our minds. It's the old story of the generous relative who cared about us when we didn't even know about him. Who included our name in his will, before we had heard his name for the first time. Suddenly you're a part of a family you never knew you had. Overnight you turn from starry-eyed dreamer into pocket-filled benefactor.

You and I both know that only in movies and fairy tales do stories like these come true. We all know that if you want anything in this life you have to work hard for it. And after working an entire lifetime, most people don't have a lot to show. Mementos and family heirlooms with little more than sentimental value are divided up every day. Most of us walk away inheriting a wealth made mostly of memories.

Even for those lucky souls that beat the impossible odds and inherit a multi-million-dollar fortune, one thing is sure . . . someone, somewhere had to work hard to amass the inheritance that would one day turn into an unexpected gift. If wishes made millionaires, we'd all be rich. But the truth is what inheritance we leave tomorrow depends on the sacrifices we make today.

Those massive inheritances that happen to a few select people in this life, depend on the sacrifices of amazingly rich and unspeakably generous great, great uncles across the ocean. It is amazing how someone's leaving this life can give us a new lease on ours. With one letter the benefactor's entire life can change in every way . . . all because they happened to be part of someone's will.

You unfold the letter and begin to read.

"Carrying his own cross, he went out to the place of the skull (which in Aramaic is called Golgotha)." "Here they crucified him, and with him two others—one on each side and Jesus in the middle."

"Pilate had a notice prepared and fastened to the cross. It read: JESUS OF NAZARETH, THE KING OF THE JEWS. Many of the Jews read this sign, for the place where Jesus was crucified was near the city, and the sign was written in Aramaic, Latin and Greek. The chief priests of the Jews protested to Pilate, "Do not write 'The King of the Jews,' but that this man claimed to be king of the Jews." Pilate answered, "What I have written, I have written."

"When the soldiers crucified Jesus, they took his clothes, dividing them into four shares, one for each of them, with the undergarment remaining. This garment was seamless, woven in one piece from top to bottom. "Let's not tear it," they said to one another. "Let's decide by lot who will get it." This happened that the Scripture might be fulfilled which said, "They divided my garments among them and cast lots for my clothing." So this is what the soldiers did."

"Near the cross of Jesus stood his mother, his mother's sister, Mary the wife of Clopas, and Mary Magdalene. When Jesus saw his mother there, and the disciple whom he loved standing nearby, he said to his mother, "Dear woman, here is your son," and to the disciple, "Here is your mother." From that time on, this disciple took her into his home."

"Later, knowing that all was now completed, and so that the Scripture would be fulfilled, Jesus said, "I am thirsty." A jar of wine vinegar was there, so they soaked a sponge in it, put the sponge on a stalk of the hyssop plant, and lifted it to Jesus' lips. When he had received the drink, Jesus said, "It is finished." With that, he bowed his head and gave up his spirit" (John 19:17-30).

Sounds pretty fantastic, doesn't it? You may not know it, but an unexpected and undeserved inheritance has come your way. You're in the will. It was no unknown relative who died, but there was a death involved. Hebrews 9:16-17 says, "In the case of a will, it is necessary to prove the death of the one who made it, because a will is in force only when somebody has died; it never takes effect while the one who made it is living."

You probably haven't gotten a letter in the mail, but never fear. Because of Jesus' sacrifice, the will is in effect and your inheritance is there for the taking. What is different about this inheritance is God requires you to have a relationship with the one who died but now lives. Jesus Christ didn't put you in the will not knowing who you were. Just the opposite, He knows your faults, your mistakes, your needs, your deepest hurts, and your most intimate joys. He put you in the will out of a deep love for you.

Hebrews 9:15 says, "For this reason, Christ is the mediator of a new covenant, that those who are called may receive the promised eternal inheritance—now that he has died as a ransom to set them free from the sins committed under the first covenant."

Your reality check is in the mail . . . it's payday. The reality is that your sins have been paid for. The reality is that you've been set free. The reality is that you have inherited eternal life. Even if some rich relative left you ten million dollars, it's not completely out of the question that, given the right circumstances, you could earn it someday on your own. The inheritance offered you by Christ can never be earned nor ever be bought.

You are the benefactor of an inheritance like no other. As a result, the same ol's aren't quite the same anymore. How much would your day be affected if you inherited that ten million? How different is your day now that you have inherited eternal life? Sure, your Monday morning routine may not change much. But when there are no more Mondays, and you come into your inheritance, you can be glad for the one who included you in His will, and made you a part of the family whose heirloom is eternal life.

Chapter Nineteen

The Gardener
John 20:1-18

*M*ary appreciated life. She loved the people around her. She often found herself staring into sunsets, and she never let a rose in bloom pass her by.

This was not the same old Mary you used to see walking with her head down and her mind plagued with trouble. Now, every day was a special occasion, every new face an opportunity for friendship, every old face a trusted friend.

Unlike before, Mary now went out of her way to bring a little sunlight into someone else's life. How could she not, after the way the light had shone into her own life and chased away the shadows that had imprisoned her soul for so long?

Mary had become well known for her numerous gifts of kindness. The vendors in the marketplace found themselves waiting for her to drop by with a kind word and a few shekels. She was a thoughtful woman. She had become good friends with the baker from whom she bought so much bread to give to the widows she visited. She had become fast friends with the fishermen due to the many grocery errands that brought her to their nets. It was a smelly job, but Mary didn't mind going the extra mile for people.

Perhaps she had become even closer friends with the gardener. She was always stopping by for a bouquet of fresh-cut flowers for the people who meant the most in her life. The gardener was not like anyone else she had ever known. Whether his latest crop was great or small, there was always a patient determination to bring life to every seed and to draw potential from every new sprout.

Each new sunrise found him hunched over his sprouts and seeds, digging relentlessly in an often unyielding clay. Yet, the gardener was not afraid to get dirty, because he knew that getting dirty was part of growing a good garden.

Mary would often pass by his garden early in the morning. She could see him kneeling in the dirt, but he was never too busy to stop and talk a while or offer some good gardening tips.

He always said, "Look out for the weeds. Weeds are in every garden." The weeds didn't have a chance to get comfortably rooted in his garden. He would quickly brandish his pruning shears, and cut them down to size.

The gardener had become well known. Stories about his beautiful garden were discussed over backyard fences for miles around. People talked about the amazing way his garden flourished. They had never seen such a lush, fruitful garden. He made it look like a wonderland. His garden was like a welcomed oasis to a thirsty traveler.

Most people don't realize just how hard it is to grow a good garden. Mary was always surprised by how easy the gardener made it look. No doubt he disguised the difficulty with his expertise. You would have thought that he had been working in that garden since before time began. The gardener did make it look easy, but his hands always gave his hard work away.

There's one sure way to tell an amateur from an expert in the garden . . . to look at his hands. A good gardener has hands that are familiar with hard work. He had the green thumb that accompanied the trade. His hands were rough and callused from constantly working in the soil. Mary could see the coarse thickness in hands as dry and cracked as the sun-baked clay of Jerusalem.

Few things were as peaceful for Mary as walking through his garden. A garden is a world of its own just before sunrise. The morning breeze carried with it the fragrance of blossoms and the whispered "good mornings" of humming crickets and singing sparrows.

The cool morning breezes brushed across her olive cheeks and through her dark hair. The sun warmed her body as her sandaled feet slowly carried her through dew-covered grass. Mary wished mornings like this would never end. She felt as if she could spend an entire day lost in the endless beauty of the gardener's magnificent handiwork.

Mary's favorite time of morning was the moment just before the dawn, when the sounds of the garden were lulled to a hush in anticipation of the rising sun. The sun would slowly peek over the horizon, and with its warm touch, awaken each blossom from its drowsy nap.

However, this morning was different. Mary didn't notice the chatter of the crickets or the singing of the sparrows. They could have been singing a symphony, but she never heard a note. There was something else on her mind. The vivid colors of the garden Mary once appreciated were now washed in a gloomy gray. Mary's mind was as cloudy as the sky that hid the sun.

She couldn't hide her tears. She didn't try. Through her sobbing, Mary could barely focus on the centerpiece of the garden. In the middle of a garden overflowing with life stood the stronghold of death. The tomb was cold and empty . . . like Mary's heart.

Mary reluctantly approached the opening in the rock. She had been there before only to find the body of Jesus missing.

Follow Me Again

She had to take just one more look, maybe in her grief she had missed something.

Mary cautiously stepped over the broken jar of spices she had brought to anoint the body. She had dropped it from the shock of finding settled dust and neatly folded grave clothes in the place of a crucified friend.

She knelt down by the displaced stone and forced her eyes to peer into the thick, hollow darkness. Mary's crying stopped at the abrupt appearance of two angels. They were both wearing white garments, so inappropriate for the occasion. One of them asked, "Why are you crying?"

"Why am I crying?" Mary thought to herself, "what a foolish question." Mary could ask a similar question of them, why were they not crying? After all, this was a tomb. Could there be any other response to death, but tears?

In her disbelief of the question, Mary took a step backward. "They have taken my Lord away," she said, "and I don't know where they have put him." Mary turned quickly to leave the tomb and bumped into, who she thought, was the gardener.

The angels' question had made perfect sense for they saw what Mary could not. They had seen, standing behind her, the one who made tears obsolete. The reason they were not crying was that they could see the Man she was looking for right over her shoulder.

Mary feared the body had been stolen by a grave robber, but before her now stood the one who had robbed the grave of its gripping power and death of its dark finality. "Sir," she pleaded with the gardener, "if you have carried Him away, tell me where you have put Him and I will get Him."

Jesus grinned from ear to ear. He gently wiped the tears from her cheek with the back of His hand. Then He rested his hands on her shoulders, looked into her eyes and said, "Mary."

Mary . . . the way He said her name broke through the

subtle disguise revealing the love she could only have heard in His voice. Mary . . . no one else could bring comfort so quickly and completely. Mary . . . she knew the voice well because it was the same voice that had set her free. It was easy for her to memorize the tones of compassion. She had heard them so many times before.

Mary had mistaken Jesus for the gardener, but it was really no mistake. She had bumped into THE Gardener. He was the same Gardener she had seen working miracles in the Jerusalem dust, growing faith from a parched heart, planting eternal seeds in a garden where a tomb once stood.

He had been a gardener from the beginning. The first garden He planted, He created out of nothing. He cultivated a paradise in Eden and planted eternity in the hearts of men. The Gardener was no stranger to dirt, in fact He was quite proficient in making something wonderful out of something useless. It was the Gardener who had formed man out of dust and set a seed in his soul.

It was this kind of seed that Paul spoke of in 1 Corinthians 15.

"But someone may ask, 'How are the dead raised? With what kind of body will they come?' How foolish! What you sow does not come to life unless it dies. When you sow, you do not plant the body that will be, but just a seed, perhaps of wheat or of something else. But God gives it a body as he has determined, and to each kind of seed he gives its own body."

"So will it be with the resurrection of the dead. The body that is sown is perishable, it is raised imperishable; it is sown in dishonor, it is raised in glory; it is sown in weakness, it is raised in power; it is sown a natural body, it is raised a spiritual body."

"If there is a natural body, there is also a spiritual body . . . . The first man was of the dust of the earth, the second man from heaven. As was the earthly man, so are those who are of the earth; and as is the man from heaven, so also are those who are of heaven. And just as we have borne the likeness of the earthly

man, so shall we bear the likeness of the man from heaven"
(1 Corinthians 15:35-38, 42-44, 47-49).

The Gardener specialized in bringing things to life. The life
that was restored to a perishable body in a garden tomb
ensured that death would no longer have the last word. To
make us eternal, the Gardener of all time had to plant a perishable seed, His Son, Jesus Christ. And ironically, that perishable
seed bloomed into a perfect flower in of all places, a garden.

There's nothing the Devil hates more than eternal gardening. He has however, planted a seed or two in his time.
Perishable seeds. Seeds of corruption, fear, and doubt. Seeds
of things that will never last . . . much like himself. That is why
he hates the imperishable, eternal seeds planted by the hands
of the Master Gardener.

The crop that is sown now will soon be harvested. One
day, the seeds He has planted will break through the ground
that has imprisoned them. They will turn their eyes toward the
risen Son. Then death will be swallowed up in victory. For
now, He stands guard at the door of the tomb, reminding us,
just like Mary, that there is no reason for tears. He reminds us
that the tomb is now empty, He is not there, He has risen. The
Gardener has come back from the dead.

You can always tell a good Gardener by His hands: green
thumb, rough, callused . . . nail-scarred. Why are you crying?
In His hands, there is nothing to fear. Why are you worried? In
His hands, there is only peace. Why do you despair? In His
hands, are the seeds of life. When the garden grows dark, and
what you're looking for you cannot find; when you look and
there's no one there, and the grave has swallowed up your
hope; dry your eyes, look around . . . you're bound to bump
into . . . the Gardener.

Chapter Twenty

Follow Me Again
John 21:1-19

*E*very handful of stones was carefully chosen from the sandy shore. The late afternoon sun yawned and stretched its arms down to the surface of the water. Reflected light ricocheted from one rocky ledge to the next. The weather was perfect.

A light breeze swept across the calm sea as seven men walked slowly by the water's edge, skipping stones. They could hear the predictable chant of the water gently lapping onto the shore. It was good to take a walk again. They had been in self-made solitary confinement, hiding in a stuffy upper room, for more than a week.

The past few weeks had been difficult. After all, it's not every day that you're suddenly made an enemy of the government, and worse than that, an enemy of the priestly pious. Although, it wasn't every day that an executed man came back to life. It's not typical for a dead man to walk and smile and eat and breath and talk and laugh. But the last several days were not normal and their events were anything but typical.

As the seven men walked, they talked about the things that had happened. Peter, James and John, Thomas, Nathanael, and two other disciples, bounced stones across the surface of the Sea of Galilee, while bouncing thoughts and comments off one another.

Their faces where much happier now than when they had stared at their dying Lord on a cross. Their hearts were much fuller now than when the tomb was full. Their vision a bit clearer now that they had seen their resurrected Lord. Even though the pieces of the puzzle fit a little more tightly now, there were still a few pieces missing.

"The Lord said He would rise from the dead and He did." Nathanael said, "He almost scared me to death, when He walked through the door in the upper room. I thought some-one would have to raise me from the dead after that one."

James spoke the question everyone was wondering, "What are we supposed to do now?" It seemed like a fair question to ask. After all, Jesus was dead and buried one day, and a few days later, decided He would drop by the ol' upper room for a chat. This had to be hard to swallow, but they all believed. Even Thomas had gotten his chance to see and believe, after the Lord appeared to him and the others a second time. They all believed, they just wondered, "What next?"

You could see the lightbulb flash on over Peter's head, "I know what I want to do now!" Peter ran around to the front of the men and faced them. As they walked forward on the shore, Peter jogged backward and presented his proposal. "I'm going fishing! What do you guys say to that?"

That wasn't a bad idea. It had been a while, hadn't it? The group agreed to join Peter on his evening fishing trip. Funny how when our minds are scrambled and we've lost our bear-ings, it seems natural to want to return to the familiar. And that's what these men did.

They returned to the Sea of Galilee. Now there was a welcomed sight. The Sea of Galilee had been their hangout, their place to work and to play. Talk about familiar. As fishermen, it was their job to know every pattern of the water, every tendency of a sometimes less than cooperative sea, every inch of shore line . . . and they did.

This sea also held some fond, life-changing memories for them. It was here that Jesus calmed the angry waves and settled hearts of disbelief. It was on this water that Jesus had walked and permitted one to join Him. Jesus had taught thousands of people from this shore. Yes, this was definitely a familiar place.

Fishing was familiar to them too. If these men knew anything, it was fishing. As they walked, they approached the boat they had ridden in time and time again. They fixed the nets and equipment, as they had a million times before. Fishing was familiar.

The bright sun once suspended over the lake had wandered off into evening, exchanging its golden light for a pale orange glow. Hours of fishing and talking took place. At first, the familiar was refreshing and fun, then the familiar became frustrating. They weren't catching a single thing! Not one fish! Soon the orange sunset disappeared and starlight sprinkled itself over the face of the water. The full moon was bright enough to cast shadows in a boat full of tired men.

It was as if the sea was keeping her fish for a reason. It was as if God had cupped His hands under the water, holding the fish in place. The fish weren't swimming, and they weren't biting.

The seven followers . . . I mean fisherman . . . took turns napping. Morning came slowly, but it was good to see it come. The more the sun peeked out, the more the thick fog melted away. The more Peter thought about having no fish after a night of hard work, the more frustrated he became.

Oh, this was familiar all right. In fact, it was too familiar. This wasn't the first time that Peter and the others had been out fishing all night and had nothing to show for it but sore backs and tired hands. This wasn't the first time that the nets had been brought up empty over and over. This wasn't the first time the familiar became frustrating.

Peter felt déjà vu. He looked at his nets and remembered. It was about two years ago, on this very lake that he had met Jesus for the first time. The nets were empty from a night of fishing, and Peter was tired. The last thing he wanted to do was go out and try again, but Jesus asked him to. To satisfy His request Peter set out for the deep.

Peter remembered trying to yank up the nets. He remembered thinking that they were caught on something. But they weren't caught on any thing, they had caught many things: fish, thousands of fish! The nets were so full, they must have lost a few hundred fish trying to get them in the boat.

He remembered being astounded by Jesus. And Peter remembered that day when he left his nets behind on the shore and followed the Savior. A lot had happened since then. Peter had followed, but he had also denied. Peter had said he would never leave, but he had abandoned ship. Peter said he would sooner die than deny, but it didn't work that way.

Peter's memory was interrupted by some smart aleck on the shore, "Did you catch anything, guys?" What kind of question is that? "No, not a thing!" someone yelled back to the man on the shore.

Peter almost lost it. "Did you catch anything!?" he mumbled to himself. The Man on the shore told them to throw the net on the other side, and try again. They did, and this time the nets were full . . . completely full!

Peter was still mumbling to himself and playing in his tackle box when John stopped what he was doing and started to laugh. "What did He say? Cast your net on the other side? It's the Lord! Peter, It's the Lord!"

Follow Me Again

Those words flooded the mind of Peter, as the fish had flooded their nets! Peter wrapped his robe around himself and darted into the water. The six men in the boat, smiling and laughing, guided the boat to shore and started to get out. Jesus was sitting there with a funny grin on His face, skipping stones on the water.

Peter warmed himself by the fire that glowed on the shore. The smell of grilled fish and hot bread made its way through the morning air. It looked like breakfast was ready.

"Bring some of your fish up here. Let's have a big breakfast this morning," Jesus said. The men were starved. Jesus fixed the meal and brought the fish and bread to them. This was by far their favorite meal. Jesus knew that. This morning it tasted better than all the meals before it. Mmmm, nothing like a fish fry with the Master. After the meal was over, they talked a while. John got up and started cleaning up the mess and tended to the fire. A few of the disciples took a brief rest on the beach.

Jesus looked at Peter and said, "Simon, son of John, do you love me more than these?" Simon? Jesus called him by his old name. Jesus had named him Peter the day he followed Him, three years ago on this same shore. Why did He call him by his old name? Maybe it was because Peter had turned again to the familiar. He had gone back to the person he was before the day he decided to follow Jesus.

"Do you love me more than these?" What is Jesus pointing to when He says that? Does Jesus point over to the other disciples, and ask, "Do you love Me more than these?" Does Jesus pick up the corner ropes of the net that was drug up on shore and ask, "Do you love Me more than these?"

What would Jesus point to if He asked you that question, "Do you love me more than these?" Would He point to a family, a wife, a title on an office door, your bank account, your church?

What would Jesus hold in His hands if He asked you, "Do you love Me more than these?" Would He hold keys to your house and sports car? Would He hold pictures of your best friends? Would He hold a wad of hundred-dollar bills?

What would you say to a question like that if you were face to face with Jesus? You would probably say exactly what Peter said. "Of course Lord, you know I love ya!" "Feed My lambs," Jesus stated and asked again, "Simon, son of John, do you love Me?"

Peter replied, "Oh, yes Lord, You know I love You."

"Take care of My sheep," Jesus answered, then questioned once more, "Simon, son of John, do you love Me?"

Peter's eyes started to tear up a little, "Yes Lord, You know everything, You know I love You!"

Jesus took Peter's hand and looked deeply into his heart, "Then feed My sheep."

Jesus had asked a strange question, but one that needed to be asked. In fact, Jesus had asked the question. The question that would answer all other questions. Do you love Me? Jesus didn't ask, "So is everything OK with you, Peter?" He didn't ask, "Are you still doing a lot of successful ministry?" No, Jesus asked, "Do you love Me?"

They talked some more. It was as if Peter had just been reinstated. Peter had a job to do for Jesus, and it didn't involve sleepless nights of dropping nets. It didn't involve the frustrating familiar. It involved the adventure of loving Him, and the feeding of a flock. It was as if Jesus had made a statement about returning to the familiar after something as life changing as death and resurrection.

Jesus had taught a lesson about the frustration of returning to the familiar. The fish weren't biting until the Master gave the word. Jesus took the familiar and made it into something fantastic, as He always did. Don't return to the familiar, not after something as fantastic as the risen Savior.

Jesus rose to His feet, and the others got up from the sand as well. Jesus picked up a perfect stone and skipped it across the calm water like nobody else could. Then He repeated the words He had said a few years ago on the same shore covered with nets and fish. Peter stared at Jesus. Jesus turned, made a step toward the sunrise and said, "Come, follow Me . . . again."

Following the Right King

Look, he is coming with the clouds, and every eye will see him, even those who pierced him; and all the peoples of the earth will mourn because of him. So shall it be! Amen. "I am the Alpha and the Omega," says the Lord God, *"who is, and who was, and who is to come, the Almighty."*

"Behold, I am coming soon! My reward is with me, and I will give to everyone according to what he has done. I am the Alpha and the Omega, the First and the Last, the Beginning and the End. "Blessed are those who wash their robes, that they may have the right to the tree of life and may go through the gates into the city. Outside are the dogs, those who practice magic arts, the sexually immoral, the murderers, the idolaters and everyone who loves and practices falsehood. "I, Jesus, have sent my angel to give you this testimony for the churches. I am the Root and the Offspring of David, and the bright Morning Star." The Spirit and the bride say, *"Come!" And let him who hears say, "Come!" Whoever is thirsty, let him come; and whoever wishes, let him take the free gift of the water of life* (Revelation 1:7-8; 22:12-17, emphasis added).

About the Authors

Scott Tucker is a teacher, preacher, writer, trainer, computer programmer, and amateur musician. He was previously the minister with Myers Christian Church and currently volunteers time (along with his wife Cathy) teaching Sunday school, performing with the praise band, and working with the drama ministry at the Brookville Church of Christ. Scott holds a Bachelor of Arts with an emphasis in preaching from Kentucky Christian College, an M.A. in Communication from Morehead State University and is currently pursuing a Ph.D. in Communication from Regent University. Additionally, Scott has been an adjunct professor for Kentucky Christian College and now for Cincinnati Bible College.

Darren Walter is the Guest Services and Volunteer Minister at Southeast Christian Church in Louisville, Kentucky. Southeast averages over 15,000 in attendance each weekend and continues to grow with God's blessing. Darren holds a Bachelor of Arts degree in Bible and Ministry with an emphasis in preaching from Kentucky Christian College, where he and his wife Amanda met. In addition to his ministry at Southeast, Darren enjoys presenting seminars and training sessions at churches around the country. Check out Darren's Web site at www.magnetministries.com. In addition to *Follow Me Again*, Darren has authored a book entitled *The People-Magnet Church* available through College Press Publishing.